SEA
ANGLING
IN IRELAND

JOHN RAFFERTY

MERCIER PRESS
WHAT YOU NEED TO READ

After a day's sea angling nothing makes a fish bigger than almost being caught, turning all fishermen into liars except you and me. And to tell you the truth, I'm not so sure about you.

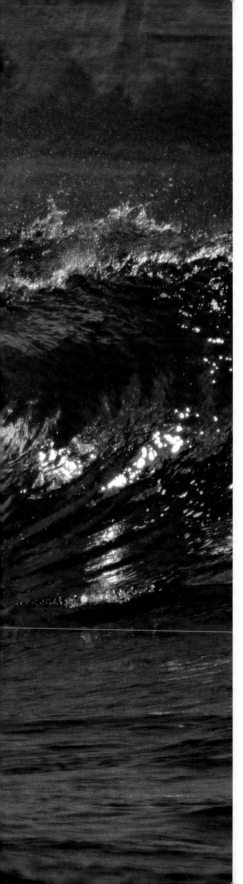

Contents

Preface

This book has evolved over the past seven years from a chaotic cluster of written notes about my sea angling escapades to what you see in front of you now, a comprehensive guide to understanding and catching some of the best sporting and eating fish that the Irish coast has to offer. Sea angling has changed dramatically over the last twenty years with some species, such as tope, turbot, cod, haddock, whiting, spur dogs, ling and plaice to name but a few, being over-fished by the commercial sector; this has now been somewhat rectified by quotas and mesh sizes.

What we must not forget is that the commercial fisherman must make a living too and, like us anglers, he wants fish stocks to remain stable to secure his and his family's future. Sea angling has also changed with the introduction of state of the art fishing rods, reels, lines and traces; no longer do we need the brush handle type rods or lines that would anchor the boat if you were unlucky enough to snag the bottom. Success is never guaranteed in this sport, there are no overstocked ponds of fish to cast a hook into, like our freshwater brethren are accustomed to, but there are some places that out-fish others time and time again.

No matter how much or how little you know about the sport of sea angling, it will always be a continual learning curve full of memorable experiences and interspersed with breathtaking scenery. The coastal landscape is always changing, with incoming tides, large waves and the occasional sunrise and sunset.

Sea angling can be divided into two sections: boat angling and shore angling; this book covers mainly boat angling, although it does have some tips for the sea angler who wishes to fish from the shore. Boat angling is rapidly growing year by year with more and more sea anglers trailing their own craft all over the country to get to the coast and their favourite fishing spots.

Sea angling from a boat is a fascinating sport that has often seen me work an eighteen-hour day just so I could have the following day off to pursue the sport I love and, indeed, the sport I grew up with. It is limitless in the variety it offers, both in the number of species and the methods used to catch them. But sea angling is more than just catching fish; it's about understanding the seasons, the best time to fish the tide, finding where the fish are more likely to lie in wait for their prey and, of course, what prey are on the menu at any given time of the day or season.

No two trips to sea are ever the same and if you are willing, something new can be learned everyday. It is not necessary to follow slavishly my instructions or anyone else's for that matter, written or otherwise. Some careful thought, several attempts by trial and error and, above all, a little patience will soon simplify every challenge you come up against regardless of what stage of proficiency you have reached. And if you, the reader, find some useful information in this book, as I trust you will, I will feel a certain satisfaction knowing that I have completed my intended task.

I would like to express my appreciation to Mr Eric Parkes at the *Irish Angler's Digest* who, many years ago, gave me my first opportunity to write a sea angling column about different fish species, their habitats, cycles and how best to go about catching them. Thanks are also due to Udarás Na Gaeltachta and the Donegal County Council for their kind sponsorship.

I am also grateful to all the charter skippers who sent me photos and kept me up to date with how their areas along the coast were fishing. Much credit must also be given to Denis Boyle, Cormac Burke and Liam Gillespie, three keen sea anglers who accompany me on many sand and reef fishing trips and who keep me on my toes where catching different species are concerned. Finally I would like to thank my wife Stella, my son Aidan and my daughter Emma, who have put up with my writing moods, good and bad, over the last few years. Thanks guys.

Réamhrá

á bunrúta an leabhair seo le fáil i gcarnán nótaí atá curtha le chéile agam faoi thurais phléisiúrtha iascaireachta atá déanta agam le seacht mbliana anuas. Tá súil agam gurb é an toradh atá ar an tsaothar seo nó treoirleabhar cuimsitheach ar iascaireacht slaite farraige. Tá sé de bhuntáiste agam gur tógadh cois cladaigh mé i Rosa Thír Chonaill, áit a bhfuil iascaireacht den scoth le fáil ar mhuir agus tír. Ó tharla gur sa Ghaeltacht is mó a dhéanaim mo chuid iascaireachta, tá leaganacha Gaeilge d'ainmneacha na n-iasc tugtha agam i ndeireadh an leabhair. Is seod luachmhar na hainmneacha dúchasacha seo d'iascaire ar bith, tá an chuid is mó acu linn le os cionn míle bliain agus bheadh sé ina thubáiste iad a ligint i ndearmad.

Tá súil agam go mbainfidh sibh sult as mo leabhar agus as an aistear farraige a bhfuil sibh ag dul ina cheann sa tsaothar seo.

Introduction

The sea covers more than two thirds of the world's surface; it influences our climate and supplies us with a large percentage of our food. Vast areas are still unexplored and new species are discovered on an almost daily basis by marine biologists; so when we go sea angling we are never entirely certain what we will catch. Sea angling is becoming increasingly popular and we are all excited by the thrill of adventure it always offers. A note of caution though – some species are in danger of becoming extinct in the near future (cod, ling, shark, blue fin tuna, to name but a few) because of over-fishing, and as anglers we must take steps, however small, to help protect those species by practising catch and release and insuring others do the same. Hopefully the day will come when no species will be in danger and all can be kept at a manageable level.

There is no closed season in sea fishing, rather it's the fish that dictate the season for the sea angler. Not all marine fish are resident in our waters throughout the year. Cod, for example, usually arrive in large numbers in October and leave in February, although some individuals do stay and can be caught throughout the year. Turbot move to deeper waters during winter months, whereas whiting move inshore during these months and to deeper waters around March and April. Mackerel usually arrive around our coast in May and stay with us until September or October. These are just a few of the species that are seasonal for the sea angler, moving closer to the shore at certain times of the year before migrating or retreating to deeper waters. There are many species within the angler's grasp all year round but different techniques, traces and baits need to be used to attract and catch them; there is always an element of unpredictability about sea angling, leaving you uncertain, never one hundred per cent sure about what has just taken the bait. When you've been sea angling a few times you'll know what I mean. My advice to you is to study and understand as much as you possibly can about the habitat, movements and the likes and dislikes of your intended quarry. Fish are intelligent; they come from an environment where one mistake can cost them their life but, on the other hand, food is at a premium and fish have to be highly aggressive to get their meal. So if you, the angler, can present your bait in a manner the fish can associate with then there's no reason why you won't catch your fair share. Taking note of dates, areas, traces, baits and techniques used to catch them will also prove to be invaluable to you on later outings. I assure you, by following this advice your catches will increase in size and quantity, turning you into a highly skilled and very proficient angler.

There are several different types of sea angling to choose from, including beach, rock, estuary, pier or boat fishing, and by and large the same, or slightly varied, tactics and baits are used. Most of my sea angling is done from a boat, so all traces and tactics are reflective of this but can easily be adapted to your particular situation. Joining a sea angling club is a good idea for the novice angler, even if it's only for a few years. Clubs usually hold competitions or league outings on a regular basis – these will help keep you up to date with the latest tackle, techniques and ideas and enhance your basic skills, in time giving you a slight edge on other anglers and, of course, the fish.

Fishing should be fun, as well as providing you and your family with the freshest and tastiest food. Entering competitions for at least a few years should significantly help you improve your fishing skills; try talking to some well known and experienced anglers, most of whom will be happy to give you a few tips. You can then apply and adapt these skills to your own fishing. Please don't make the mistake of becoming too competitive or competition minded, however; if you do it can start to feel more like a job than a leisurely pursuit and will eventually destroy the intense pleasure that sea angling and catching fish can give.

Safety First

Basic common sense applies when you are going to sea. First and foremost it must be respected at all times. The greatest risks to anyone who falls into the sea off our coast are death by hypothermia and drowning. Even during the warmest summers our sea temperatures never rise very high; some-one immersed in the water, even for a short period of time, can become cold very quickly and incapable of helping themselves as they succumb to hypothermia. My advice is to go on a one day Basic Sea Survival Course; most of it is common sense as sea survival is all about suitable equipment, adequate preparation and knowledge of survival techniques. Always check the tide before collecting bait or fishing; if it's not

You never know what you might encounter on a fishing trip

favourable then don't go, as any mistake made at sea is often fatal. Remember, the sea is not our friend nor is it our enemy. It can be either to us at any time; it can give you a record-breaking fish and crush you with the same wave.

If you are going fishing with your own boat, safety checks need to be carried out on the morning of every trip. These checks need to be done thoroughly, so get into a routine and stick to it; it only takes a few minutes.

1. Always make sure that you have more than enough fuel on board to last you the day.

Safety First: handheld VHF, mobile phone in a waterproof cover, flares and lifejacket or PFD (Personal Flotation Device)

2. Check that your handheld VHF is charged and working correctly. Also, carry a mobile phone in a waterproof cover as an emergency backup; don't rely on a mobile phone for distress communications at sea.

3. Examine the flares and confirm that they are not out of date. There are three types of flares – orange, red and rocket parachute. Orange smoke flares are for day use only and can be seen up to 4 kilometers away on a clear day. Red handheld flares are for night use and can be seen up to 10 kilometers away. Rocket parachute flares can reach a height of 300 metres and are used for longer range attention seeking. All flares only burn for about one minute so only use them when other boats and planes are in the area.

4. Most boating fatalities involve small craft so make sure your life-jacket or PFD (Personal Flotation Device) is in good working order, is serviced every year and has a whistle attached; more than 80 per cent of boating fatalities are caused by not wearing a PFD.

5. Always dress warmly, as the weather can change quickly at sea. Make sure the outer layer is brightly coloured so that you are more visible to rescuers should the worst happen.

6. A good survival suit is essential for the winter months or if you are fishing offshore. If the unthinkable happens and you end up in the water, the survival suit may mean the difference between life and death. Avoid unnecessary swimming to help conserve energy and body heat until help arrives.

7. During hot summer days wear sun cream and a hat to avoid the worst of the sun's rays and drink plenty of water. Whenever you go fishing take a good packed lunch and a non-alcoholic drink in a flask, as you will feel hungry after a few hours. Remember – your own safety is paramount, so

no matter how good the fishing is, if weather conditions seem to be worsening, pack up and go home; all too often we hear of anglers getting lost needlessly, so pay attention, be careful and survive.

When to go Fishing

Twice a day the sea level rises and falls, caused by the gravitational pull of the moon. The times for high and low water vary from day to day and also vary at different places around the coast. You can check the state of the tide in local papers, angling magazines, purpose made tide books and on the internet.

A big part of being successful at sea angling is down to good planning and having a clear understanding of fish behaviour. Whether it's shore, rock or boat angling, local knowledge of the area is vital if you are to succeed. There is no substitute for local knowledge; check with local tackle shops, talk to them and ask them about local angling clubs and try to get contact details for club committee members who might talk to you.

Arranmore lifeboat on exercises

Most anglers will send you in the right direction, telling you where to catch the best fish and what dangers to watch out for. Sea anglers will often refer to a particular area as a 'mark', a spot where anglers regularly catch fish. The fish congregate at these marks for a number of reasons; usually it's a reef, rocky outcrop, shellfish bed, an old wreck or a sandbank that provides a hiding place from predators, and allows the fish to stay in groups of their own species. This means safety in numbers and, of course, a good supply of food. On an inshore mark, if the water is shallow you will generally only catch small fish but larger fish will come and go at different stages of the tide while they hunt their prey. On a mark in deeper water, bigger fish will be resident here all the time as there is less light here and it is the perfect place for a surprise attack on their prey. While fishing on reefs, rough ground or sandbanks inshore I find that the best time for fishing is about two hours before high or low water and about one hour after slack water. These times can be lengthened during big spring tides.

Fishing on Reefs

2

Whether you have your own boat or are going with others on a charter boat, reef fishing will offer you a whole range of species, which you can catch if the right baits and tactics are used. Inshore and offshore reefs are excellent fishing marks; their gullies and ledges will hold many of the best sporting species. First you need to choose a particular reef; most will have the potential to hold several species. The next decision to be made by you or the skipper is whether to drift or anchor over the reef or divide up your day and do a bit of both. Anchoring is probably the best option if you are looking for different species, as drifting will limit you to two or three species on most days. Reefs are very similar to wrecks for holding fish; they are ideal for providing the sanctuary that fish need from currents and predators. Smaller baitfish use the reef for cover and

A good pollack caught while reef fishing

for safety, while bigger fish congregate at the reef for shelter and to feed on the baitfish. There are several countries around the world, including the USA and Spain, that are currently running grant-aided programmes to facilitate the construction of artificial reefs to help conserve fish stocks in areas where numbers have declined drastically as a result of over-fishing. The US army has given large numbers of decommissioned tanks, old aircraft carriers and artillery for the schemes. Some of the artificial reefs are now teeming with life, proving that these types of projects can and do work.

Freshly caught mackerel

A wide range and good supply of bait is essential for a successful day's reef fishing. If at all possible, collect your own bait; this not only guarantees you top quality bait but will also save you a lot of money in the long term. Top of the bait list are sand eels, which predatory fish will eagerly take on the reef. Sand eels commonly shoal on or around reefs; mackerel and ragworm or lugworm are also excellent baits when they're in top condition. Sand eels are used to catch pollack slightly above the top of the reef and can also be used to hook the occasional coalfish, cod or ling. Worms are necessary if you want to catch wrasse, while mackerel is essential bait for catching ling and conger at the bottom of the reef (sometimes during the summer months fresh mackerel can be caught on reefs). Just off the reef there is the possibility of catching a bonus brill or even a turbot. The most important thing to remember for a successful day's reef fishing is that the bait must be as fresh as possible, and in the case of worms, they must be alive.

Anchoring

If you are angling from a charter boat then you won't have to worry about getting anchored over a reef correctly; the skipper will know how to do this.

If you are out on your own boat, however, anchoring can be a little trickier. A fish finder or some form of sounder is of great benefit in showing you when a reef begins to rise. There is a good range of fish finders on the market at present, which are of high quality and relatively cheap; you will easily re-coup your outlay on fish catches. Make sure your anchor has more than enough rope attached; this will allow you to drop your anchor on the reef as it begins to

Fish finder

rise, and you can fish the top of the reef for pollack, wrasse and coalfish. And by letting out more anchor rope you can fish the downward side of the reef and the seabed for ling and conger.

Sea angling is an enjoyable sport for all ages

Drifting

Drifting over the reef is an excellent way of catching pollack, coalfish and the occasional cod and ling. My tactic for drifting over reefs is as follows: first, using my fish finder I find the top or the highest point on the reef. Then using a plastic bottle or an old buoy (a two-litre 7-UP bottle is easily seen) I tie on a 12 ounce weight and enough string to reach the highest point of the reef. This float will mark the top of the reef. I just drift past the bottle at different distances until I establish where the fish are; once you find where they are gathering it is very simple to judge your drift each time by looking at the distance between you and your float. On a windy day or in strong tidal conditions there will be a fast drift over the reef. Pollack will strike your bait much harder than normal and will hook themselves almost every time, no strike necessary. If you see other buoys around the reef then this will usually mean that another fisherman has either nets or pots on the reef, so be careful and try to avoid the area that the fisherman is fishing; otherwise

A pot fisherman

your tackle losses will be high from snagging on his gear. Reef fishing is an excellent way of catching a number of species without having to move about too much. Once you fish on a reef a few times you will build up a mental picture of how the reef rises and falls from your weight hitting on the bottom; this will help you keep your tackle losses to a minimum and will also let you target individual species.

Fishing on Sand

3

Sand fishing was once classed as a summer sport only, but now with the change in seasons and mild winters, sand fishing can be carried out almost all year round. I have to say that sand fishing is probably my favourite type of fishing, not just because of the quality of eating fish that you catch but because it's so relaxing. You don't have to be on your guard to prepare to strike at every bite; with sand fishing you can sit back and give the fish plenty of time to take your bait. Large areas of sand can be fished with limited success, but a sandbank will hold large concentrations of a variety of different sand dwellers, which use the bank as their natural larder as well as a safe haven. Sandbanks are caused by tidal activity and are found offshore as well as inshore. They vary in depth and have channels and gullies, in which the larger fish lie in wait for their food to be carried along on the currents. Small sandbanks are excellent places to fish if you have your own boat, as they are less likely to be targeted by commercial trawlers. Sandbanks will

A good place for decent flatfish

hold a variety of species, including turbot, brill, plaice, sole, dab, flounder, bass, dogfish, tope, ray, whiting and grey, red and tub gurnard; even wrasse and pollack make an appearance here when there's an abundance of sand eels and baitfish around. Congers can also be caught at night. Once you locate the sandbank you want to fish, you need to check to see if you are able to drift over it. Drifting is the best way to fish on the sand as it allows you to cover vast areas of ground and presents you with the opportunity to offer bait to the fish in a natural way with the aid of tidal currents. Strong tides or winds may cause the boat to drift too fast, making it almost impossible to keep your trace on the bottom; in these conditions anchoring is the only viable option.

Anchoring on sandbanks

Anchored on a sandbank

Anchoring over the sandbank correctly requires a good deal of skill. Getting the anchor to hold can be tricky at times; a useful tip is to put extra rope on the anchor, which can be played out to allow you to fish down the edge of the sandbank. Ideally, the boat needs to be positioned over the downward side of the bank ; this is where the fish lie to avoid the strong currents while waiting for their prey to get washed helplessly towards them. Anchoring the boat over the top of the bank will still allow you to catch fish, but only in small quantities compared to what could be caught on the downward side of the bank.

Baits for sand fishing

Baits for sand fishing should be the same type of food the fish expect to find on or in the sand. Lugworm, ragworm, razor fish, cockles, clams, mussels, squid and sand eels are the usual sand fishing baits. My favourites are sand eels, lugworm and squid; these three baits have given me more success than any of the other baits I've used. Sand eels or fillets of sand eels are absolutely brilliant for catching all sand species, especially the larger turbot and brill. Bait for sand fishing should be as fresh as possible. In the case of lugworm and ragworm, these should be alive if possible. The exception to using fresh bait for sand fishing is when you are fishing for dab; on occasion, dab seem to prefer bait

Lugworms and cockles

that is not fresh but quite stale. I have had good catches of dab on worms that were several days old and even when using leftover lugworms and ragworms which had been frozen. The downside to using stale bait is that you will also attract more dogfish.

Tackle for sand fishing

Light rods and reels are all you need for sand fishing; 20 pound class gear will be more than sufficient to tackle any of the larger fish. If the area is known for only smaller fish then 12 pound to 15 pound class spinning gear is adequate to let the fish show a little bit of their fighting ability. There are several different traces which can be used when fishing over sand; a favourite of mine, especially if there is a good showing of dab, is the large double spreader bar, which is also great for beginners as there is little chance of your trace tangling in slack tides. Long flowing traces baited with live sand eel are great for hooking brill, turbot and ray, as well as the occasional large plaice.

Fishing at sunset at Arranmore Island

One up and two down traces with beads and a large spoon at the end will also take some beating on days when things are less than frenzied. Whichever trace you use, always remember never to be in a rush to strike at fish while fishing on the sand; a good tip is to leave your rod standing against the side of the boat or in the rod holder, with the reel in free spool and the ratchet on, and just watch for the bites at the top of the rod.

On my first day angling on the sand several years ago, an experienced angler told me: 'Once you see a bite on your rod let out line and wait for around thirty seconds; then engage the reel, tighten the line and lift the rod to set the hook.' No doubt most seasoned sand anglers have their own techniques but this method works well for me.

Fishing on Rough/ Broken Ground

Very few parts of the seabed are completely flat or consist of totally clear barren ground. The seabed is as varied for the fish as land is for us, consisting of flat areas of sand and mud, large pinnacles of rocks and huge areas of flat rock and loose stone interspersed with reefs and small patches of sand that attract a variety of fish. Gaps between the stones and gravel provide the perfect sanctuary for small fish, crabs, hermit crabs, winkles, limpets, mussels and marine worms, which are the preferred food of bigger fish.

Areas of broken ground on the seabed that are in close proximity to a sand bank can be a safe haven for flatfish whenever trawlers are towing on the bank; indeed, small patches of sand in the middle of rough ground will sometimes have an abundance of prime flatfish of exceptional size. Big pollack, coalfish, conger, ling and even wrasse will leave the safety of the

Plaice are commonly caught on rough ground

reef to patrol over the rough ground in search of food. Plaice are commonly caught on rough ground in areas where there is a mussel bed nearby. Several members of the ray family and spur dogs can also be caught here during their quest for a meal.

On the Ground

Areas of broken ground that are rarely fished will prove fruitful for the sea angler who adopts the appropriate tactics. These areas do not have to be very big to hold large concentrations of fish and can be found easily enough with the aid of a fish finder or during the summer months by looking to see where the local lobster fishermen have set their pots. Set lobster pots are good indicators for broken ground but remember not to fish too close to the pots or your gear may become entangled in them. When fishing over rough ground, a 'rotten bottom' should always be attached between the trace and the weight (a rotten bottom is a small piece of weaker line than that of the trace line); in the event of you snagging on the bottom the rotten bottom will give way, leaving your trace intact but just needing a weight.

TIP

Instead of weaker line I like to use a paper clip between the trace and the weight; if the weight snags then the paper clip is easily straightened and lets go of your weight. Some anglers use old spark plugs as weights to cut down on costs but if you make your own weights then you don't mind losing a few.

Traces for fishing over rough ground

Certain types of traces work better than others when it comes to fishing over rough ground. My personal favourites are two up and one down rigs, two hooks above a pirk and a double spreader. The two up one down rig is simple enough; the two snoods above the weight are about six inches long with a few beads and a small pear-shaped spoon about the size of your thumbnail. Directly above the weight I like to use a six-inch wire boom to which I attach 12 to 18 inches of 30 pound mono and at the end of the mono I like to attach a spinner like the red and silver ones you might use to spin for mackerel. I change the hook on the spinner according to the size of

Mackerel type spinner

Artificial eel   Cuckoo wrasse

fish that I'm looking for. If it's ling or pollack I'll use around a 4/0 to 6/0 black Aberdeen hook and if it's gurnard, ray, wrasse, cuckoo wrasse or most of the flatfish species then I will use a 2/0 to a 3/0 black Aberdeen. On the double spreader I use between 12 and 18 inches of mono with beads, spoons and hooks; the hooks vary in size according to the size of the intended targets. The double spreader in effect gives you two flowing traces where you can try a different bait on each hook to see which bait is the particular favourite with the fish that day. Spinning with a lead head and a jelly worm, artificial eel or mackerel strip over rough ground can be very productive at times, especially if pollack, coalfish or cod are there in any numbers.

Tackle for rough/broken ground fishing

My hook preference is always for a Kamazan B940; these are chemically sharpened and result in excellent hook-ups even in the toughest mouths. The only time I use a different hook is when I am using a pirk, then I will use a stainless steel hook in a size 6/0 or bigger. Rods and reels do not have to be heavy duty for most rough ground fishing unless you are going to anchor and try for congers. Twenty pound gear is sufficient for all other species over this ground. I like to use braid on a 20 pound Ugly Stik rod and a Penn 25GLS lever drag reel; the braid gives me a great deal of sensitivity to the hook and the softness of the rod allows the fish to fight hard without pulling the hook out of its mouth. Also, the lever drag allows me to apply and ease the pressure on the fish with my thumb during the fight.

Baits

A selection of baits will help you catch a good variety of species over rough ground. Fresh mackerel and sand eels are probably the main baits you will

require, while lugworm and/or ragworm will tempt some of the flatfish, wrasse and gurnard. Strips of squid used in a cocktail are excellent, and sand eels are a must if you are looking to catch any amount of pollack. Peeler, hermit crabs, winkles and mussels will tempt the most fickle of fish to your hook but make sure you attach them with bait elastic otherwise you will spend most of your time retrieving your trace to replace the bait on the hooks.

Periwinkles are excellent bait

TIP Try a different bait on each hook on the trace when starting your day's fishing; once you discover which bait or combination of baits is consistently successful then fish it on all the hooks.

Fishing on Wrecks

5

Weather is probably the most important factor in wreck fishing; bad weather usually means you cannot travel offshore to where the best wreck fishing is found. These wrecks are typically untouched for months at a time, resulting in large numbers of prime fish. Wreck fishing is generally considered a summer sport, and is not for the faint-hearted, but it is the most likely place for any sea angler to go who is looking to catch a specimen or a potential record-breaking fish. Weather conditions need to be settled to allow the charter boats to travel the sometimes vast distances to the chosen wreck; up to two-thirds of your time is often spent travelling to

The seabed all along the Irish coast is littered with wrecks

and from the wreck site. Once there, excessive depths must be conquered to reach the wreck and then hopefully the arm-wrenching battle with the big fish from the abyss will begin. Normally, wreck fishing is only done by seriously experienced anglers with specialised gear for the job. The seabed all along the Irish coast is littered with wrecks of all sizes courtesy of two World Wars and our adverse weather conditions. A few of these wrecks are better known because of the circumstances surrounding their sinking, loss of life or the cargo they were carrying. Probably our two most famous wrecks are the

Taking shelter in a quiet cove during a storm

Lusitania off the old head of Kinsale, which was torpedoed during the First World War and sank with the loss of 1,195 lives, and the *Laurentic*, which hit a mine at the mouth of Lough Swilly and sank in 1917 carrying 3,211 gold bars valued today at approximately €375 million. Newly discovered or infrequently visited wrecks are the best ones for anglers as they will usually hold the most fish.

All the wrecks along our coast have become home for fish and some of these fish have become very large indeed within the relative safety of the wreck. Competition for food among these fish can become intense, which makes them excellent sport for the angler. Finding wrecks has become easier with the aid of satellite navigation systems, high quality sounders and an increasing number of sophisticated charter boats.

Positioning the boat over the wreck is the skipper's job; an experienced skipper will be capable of giving the anglers a good drift over the wreck, or anchoring over it so that the anglers' traces are falling towards the area of the wreck where the fish have congregated. It may take the skipper a few attempts to get the best position, so bear with him or her while they complete this tricky task.

Tackle for wreck fishing

The tackle required to go wreck fishing must be heavy duty; nothing less than 50 pound class should be used. Remember that fish here are almost always bigger than those caught on the inshore reefs. Your reel should be a good quality brand, one that is fit for the job, and should be serviced on a regular basis. The line on the reel also needs to be of superior quality. I like to use braid, which lets me feel every bite no matter how soft it is. It also allows me to feel my weight when it touches the wreck, and lets me use a lighter weight than would be possible if I was using mono.

The only downside with using braid is that, if you tangle with another angler on the boat, the usual outcome is that one of you has to cut your line. On the end of the line a good quality swivel should be used to attach the line to the trace; the trace should be simple and straightforward.

Spider wire braid

Simplicity is critical when wreck fishing, the less intricate your trace the less chance of becoming entangled on the wreck, keeping your gear losses and costs to a minimum. Only use one hook or two at the very most on your trace because of the size and quality of the fish. Use more than two hooks and you're asking for trouble. If you're drifting over the wreck then a flowing trace is probably the best rig to use, but if you are anchoring then a heavy mono or a wire trace is essential as congers will soon bite through anything lighter.

Hooks need to be top quality and sizes need to be at least a 6/0 or bigger. Weights of up to two pounds and sometimes more have to be used depending on a few factors: you need more weight if the water is very deep, if you're using mono instead of braid, if you're drifting over the wreck instead of anchoring or if there's a strong run of tide at the wreck.

Baits for wreck fishing

The main baits required for wreck fishing are mackerel, sand eels and squid. Sand eels are excellent on a flowing trace for pollack, coalfish and cod, as are long back strips and belly strips of mackerel. If anchored, mackerel flappers or whole squid will take some beating for congers and ling. Artificial eels and jelly worms are also very successful on the wreck for pollack, coalies, cod and the occasional ling. Pirks, either shop bought or home made, also work well sometimes, while the inclusion of a large mackerel fillet on the pirk can make all the difference. A sink and lift movement needs to be applied when using a pirk

Freshly caught sandeels

without bait. A lot of wrecks lie on a sandy seabed so the prospect of a large turbot around the vessel is always on the cards. Some unusual species of fish turn up on the deeper offshore wrecks; these include torsk, bluemouth rock-fish, triggerfish, stone basse, wreckfish and redfish to name but a few.

Conservation

Large amounts of fish can be caught from wrecks. Remember that most fish suffer depth changes poorly when taken quickly from even moderate depths and they will often suffer from a greatly distended swim bladder, leaving them trashing helplessly on the surface to die. A slower rate of retrieval once you get the fish clear of the wreck greatly increases its chances of survival; this will also cut down on the chances of ripping the hook from the fish's mouth and losing it.

Triggerfish

Clockwise: Torsk, bluemouth rockfish, stone basse, wreckfish

TIP

Heavy duty gear is essential, nothing less than 50lb class should be used while wreck fishing, ask the skipper for advice on what to use and what equipment is required for your day out.

SPECIES

Pollack

6

P ollack (*Pollachius Pollachius*) is the most likely medium sized fish that any sea angler will encounter while out for a day's fishing. These fish are capable of growing to over 20 pounds in weight; the Irish record stands at 19 pounds 3 ounces but a specimen is 12 pounds or over. They provide superb sport on light tackle and even a small pollack will give a good fight if it is given a chance with light gear. Fishing pollack with a rod, reel and line of 50 pound class will mean that all the odds are stacked in the angler's favour and the fish will not be able to show its true fighting potential. But go fishing pollack on 12 pound class gear or even lighter, and now skill takes over from luck, such as when you get a bite and a fish takes several yards of your line and trace towards the bottom in as many seconds. Pollack are active hunters and are capable of sudden bursts of terrific speed. If they are caught in shallow water and on light gear it will get the adrenaline rushing in even the most experienced anglers. This is what sport fishing is all about.

A specimen pollack caught on a lead head

Bait, tactics and traces for fishing pollack are as wide ranging as the fish they are meant to catch, although there are some that stand out above all the others.

I have a few favourite ways of fishing for pollack – the flowing trace, spinning with a lead head and spinning with a lead ball shot. The flowing trace is the most successful method I have used and has proven to be more consistent at catching pollack than any other. This consists of a hollow plastic boom fed onto the main line, followed by a plastic bead and then a snap swivel.

The plastic bead acts as a shock absorber between the boom and the snap swivel. The trace itself should consist of at least 8 feet of mono, going as far up as 18 feet. I usually use around 12 feet of mono to the hook. The hook is one of the most important pieces of equipment when fishing, but is something that a lot of anglers take for

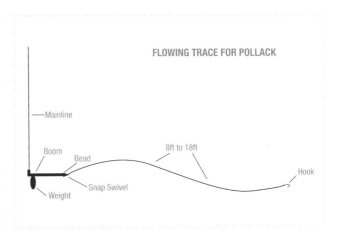

FLOWING TRACE FOR POLLACK

Mainline

Boom

Bead

8ft to 18ft

Snap Swivel

Weight

Hook

granted. Rusted and blunt hooks must be dumped. Every time I go fishing I use a new hook. My hook preference for catching pollack is a Kamazan B940 in sizes from 3/0 to 6/0. These hooks are chemically sharpened and are very strong. Care should be taken when handling chemically sharpened hooks; by the time you feel the jab on your hand it has already gone too far in to be removed by anyone other than a doctor, as many a hook-shy angler can tell you.

Now decisions must be made on what to put on the hook – artificial lures or bait. I will always favour bait as it has scent as well as movement. My first choice for bait is sand eels but some days ragworm will out-fish sand eels, especially in the earlier months of the year. Other times a thin back strip or belly strip of mackerel will take some beating. Putting the sand eel on the hook can be done in several ways; I prefer to put the hook all the way through both eyes and then nick it through the top of the back. Another way is to just pass it through both eyes.

If you are going to use live sand eels then you should only lip hook them through the bottom jaw. Free lining is the best way to fish live sand eels and the takes from the pollack are ferocious because of the

Chemically sharpened hooks

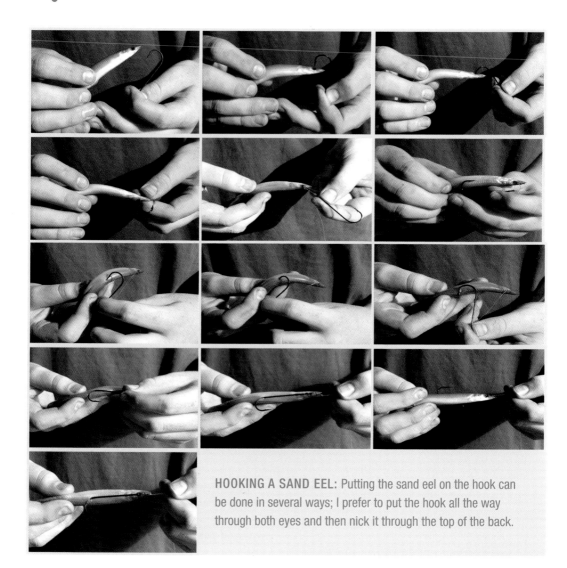

HOOKING A SAND EEL: Putting the sand eel on the hook can be done in several ways; I prefer to put the hook all the way through both eyes and then nick it through the top of the back.

sand eel diving about in an effort to escape. Other baits that are often used for catching pollack are mussels, shrimps, squid strips, sprats and herring.

Fishing artificially is another very successful way to catch pollack. Artificial eels, especially red gills, can prove very successful on any given day. The only thing that can fish better than artificial eels are the live sand eels that they are designed to imitate. Jelly worms are another great artificial lure

Artificial eels

for catching pollack. There are thousands of different types of worms but Berkeley's fire tails are one of the favourites among sea anglers.

Before you begin fishing with your flowing trace make sure that the drag on your reel is set correctly. A drag system that is set too tight will definitely lose you fish as well as your trace. The reasons for a lightly set drag will become all too apparent after you hook a pollack. Once he feels the hook he heads off towards the bottom on a very powerful run and this is where your reel must be able to give him line under some tension. Lever drag reels are fantastic for pollack fishing; the drag can be easily adjusted with your thumb as you fight the powerful fish.

It's time now to put the trace in the water and then the weight and boom; keep the boom just below the surface. You must give your trace enough time to straighten out across the surface before you let it go to the bottom at a nice steady rate; let it go too quickly and it will end up twisted around the mainline and you will waste valuable fishing time untangling it. If you're using sand eels or mackerel watch out for the seagulls lifting them. Once you feel your weight hit the bottom or your line going slack it is time to start reeling in.

The speed at which you retrieve varies from day to day depending on the fish, so it is all trial and error until you feel a bite. If you feel a bite and you are using artificial eels or jelly worms just keep reeling until you feel the weight of the fish before you strike, but if you are using bait and you feel a bite then stop reeling. To strike at this stage would be a big mistake; pollack will often hit their food to stun it before picking it up headfirst and then swallowing it. Strike when you feel the weight of the fish on the rod in the form of a heavy pull as though you were stuck on something. A lot of the time the pollack will hook itself as it crash dives towards the bottom after feeling the hook.

Once the fish feels it is hooked, its initial burst of speed is virtually unstoppable. This is where a correctly set drag will win or lose you the fish. After this first run the pollack has little stamina left and each run after the first gets weaker and weaker.

After a few minutes your fish should be on or near the surface. You must remember that your boom may be at the tip of the rod but the fish will still be another 12 feet away. A good landing net is a must in any boat; if you do not have a landing net then do not try to lift the pollack directly into the boat by the line. This is all right with a small fish but the weight of a larger pollack will mean that the hook gets ripped out of the fish's mouth once it is lifted clear of the surface. To lift the fish in without a net you must get it alongside the boat and then get your fingers under its gill covers. If you have played the fish out properly this should be no problem.

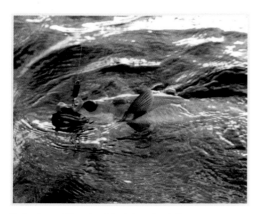
Spinning with a lead head and a jelly worm

Spinning with a lead head and a jelly worm attached is a method I use regularly for catching pollack. There is less skill required for spinning than for fishing with the flowing trace, which means that spinning is a more suitable way to show children and novices how to catch fish. It is also a very exciting way to catch pollack. All that's required for this type of fishing is a lead head and a jelly worm. The lead head is around an ounce to an ounce and a half in weight and is simply a hook with lead moulded on to it in such a way that the hook sits upright in the water. The reasons for this is to keep the hook from snagging on the bottom and to give it a better hook-up in the fish's mouth.

The jelly worm you feed on to the hook can be any colour or shape. A fire tail worm is a favourite of mine, although every angler has his or her own

The pollack will usually chase the jelly worm until he catches it

preferences. Once you have made your selection, attach the lead head directly to the mainline on your spinning rod. All lead heads have different shapes for particular motion in the water, so for this reason do not use a swivel as this would diminish movement.

Before you cast out your lead head always check that the drag is set correctly on your spinning reel. Then cast out your lead head and give it time to sink to the bottom. Once it's on the bottom you can start your retrieve. The speed of the retrieve is determined by trial and error but once you feel a bite keep retrieving at the same speed. The pollack will usually chase the jelly worm until he catches it, and occasionally you can see them right on the surface before they take. Strike when you feel the weight of the fish, and let the fight begin. There is great sport in fishing pollack this way; using bait instead of, or in addition to, the jelly worm can add to the lead head's effectiveness.

Always check the line on your trace just above the hook of the lead head for bite marks. The pollack sometimes takes the bait straight down into its stomach, leaving your line in the way of its small but sharp teeth. If it appears even slightly worn, cut off the hook or lead head and a couple of inches of line and re-tie. Care should also be taken when removing a hook that is well inside the fish's mouth, as the small cuts that you can receive from the fish's teeth on your fingers can be painful.

Very light lead heads are sometimes used for fishing with ragworms. The ragworm is hooked through the head then cast out and let sink to the bottom.

The pollack often takes the sand eel as it descends to the bottom

A lot of the time the ragworm is taken by the pollack on its way to the bottom; if it is not you can begin to retrieve it slowly until you feel a bite, then stop and wait until you feel the weight of the fish before you strike. Ballan wrasse, cuckoo wrasse and small coalies are also caught as a by-catch when fishing this way, but you need to be quick if you feel the distinctive bite of a wrasse. Reel in quickly or else the wrasse will take you to the bottom and in through the weed and then you can kiss your lead head and your wrasse goodbye.

Here's another simple trace that I like to use for fishing for pollack, one that has proven itself time and time again. It consists of a one ounce ball shot weight (with the hole through the centre) running freely on the mainline followed by a bead; at the end of the mainline a swivel is tied on. At the other end of the swivel I like to use about four or six feet of line finished off with a Kamazan B940 size 4/0 hook with a sand eel on it. This rig is used for spin-

ning and when it's cast out the ball shot starts to sink rapidly while working its way back along the outgoing mainline. This allows the sand eel and hook to descend to the seabed much slower than the ball shot. When the ball shot hits the bottom the hook and sand eel may only be half way down, so once you start to retrieve your line the sand eel has to head towards the seabed until it catches up with the weight before

This type of fishing has become very successful for me

There are plenty of other ways of catching pollack: spinning with plugs, fly-fishing

rising towards the surface with the ball shot. A lot of the time the pollack will take the sand eel as it descends to the bottom. This type of fishing has become very successful for me, especially on days when we have clear calm conditions and the fish seem easily spooked.

There are plenty of other ways of catching pollack: these include the simple three up method, trolling a lure after the boat, spinning with plugs, float fishing and, when conditions are right, fly-fishing.

Late in the evening, as night approaches, the pollack move up in the water much closer to the surface and can sometimes be seen splashing on the top of the water as they feed on

Catching pollack with a fly-rod

sand eels or small fry; this is when you can catch them on a fly-rod.

The technique for catching pollack with a fly-rod is the same as that used for catching salmon or trout. However, the fly needs to be slightly bigger than that used in freshwater, and you also need to use a sinking tip on your fly line.

The fly I use is made with a white turkey feather; when it is wet it is about three inches long and as it comes through the water it looks remarkably like a small sand eel. Great care must be taken when fishing pollack this way, as fingers can get badly hurt on the fly-reel or on the line as the fish takes the bait, screaming towards the bottom.

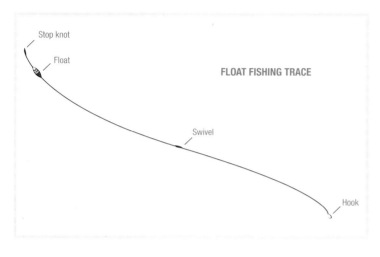

Stop knot

Float

FLOAT FISHING TRACE

Swivel

Hook

For float fishing at sea a sliding float rig works best. Slide your float on to your mainline with a small stop knot to cock it. Rubber power gum used by freshwater fish-ermen makes a great stop knot; being soft, it can be moved up or down the line without damaging it. Float fishing is carried out in fine weather; if it's windy you cannot see the float unless it is quite large and these have a tendency to alarm a taking fish to such an extent that the fish drops the bait long before the hook can be struck home. I find that fishing with an elongated float with a tube through the centre works really well and, more often than not, the float disappears with a real bang.

These are just some of the methods used for fishing pollack. Whichever you choose, always remember to fish with as light a tackle as you are comfort-able with and let the fish have a chance to fight back; this way you are assured of a good day's sport.

TIP

Pollack are a highly predatory fish so with this in mind make sure you present your lure or bait to the fish in as lifelike a man-ner as possible to ensure a successful catch rate.

Cod

od *(Gadus morhua)* is the largest of the *Gadidae* family; defined by having a single barbule under the chin. There are two clearly defined types of cod in our waters – the yellow cod and the red cod. Both are true cod; the only difference is that the yellow cod migrates between Arctic waters and Ireland annually, while the red cod remains here for an indeterminate period of time. Commercially caught cod have been weighed in excess of 150 pounds. The Irish record for a rod-caught cod stands at 42 pounds, but a specimen is a fish of 20 pounds or over. A cod caught with rod and line off the coast of New Hampshire weighed in at an amazing 98 pounds 12 ounces.

Yellow cod

As one of the most commercially sought after fish in the world, it is little wonder that cod stocks are at an all time low with the possibility of extinction in some over-fished areas. Another factor in the decline of cod numbers is the depletion of the huge herring shoals which once roamed our coastline in the 1970s and 1980s. Today these shoals are only a small fraction of what they once were and it is now believed that the cod will never be able to return to sustainable numbers unless the herring are allowed to do so first. A ban on cod fishing in some areas and at certain times is in place; the protected areas are usually known spawning grounds for cod. In good spawning years cod numbers can increase dramatically and hopefully this species will begin to recover and once again become a common sight among the angler's catch.

Red cod

Cod is also the number one target for anglers. Every angler who has ever caught a cod, even a small one, has felt a certain satisfaction. Although not renowned for their fighting qualities, good cod have a tendency when hooked to use their sheer body weight and bucket-sized mouths to hold against the tide, giving the angler the feeling of being snagged on something other than the bottom. Cod are often called the dustbins of the sea, because some of the items removed from the stomachs of gutted cod are almost unbelievable. Large stones, squashed beer and mineral cans, plastic cups and even empty shotgun cartridges. Cod have an enormous appetite and will eat almost anything in the sea. Shellfish and marine worms are the main baits used by anglers when trying to catch these fish. But cod that move offshore are more at home with a diet of fish. Top baits for cod are peeler crab, lugworm, ragworm, razor fish, shrimps, squid, sprats, herring, pouting, sand eel and mackerel. A cocktail of any of these baits will also prove successful. Every angler that I know has a favourite bait and tactic for catching cod and no two seem to be exactly the same.

TOP BAIT: Shrimp

Artificial lures are also an excellent way of catching cod, with red gills, jelly worms and hokkais the most effective. But the chrome-finished pirk is the most successful of all, especially over wrecks and offshore reefs. The first of these pirk-type lures were invented by Scandinavian fishermen for catching cod, ling and pollack. They comprised simply of a shiny lead covered with hooks, known as a ripper. There are now thousands of pirks on the market, in many different shapes and sizes.

A cod caught on razorfish

Homemade pirks are also very effective and are much cheaper than shop-bought ones. Cheap pirks are needed if you are fishing over rough ground or on wrecks where tackle losses will be quite high (see next chapter for instructions on making pirks). Your pirk must be on or near the bottom in order to catch cod, as they are a bottom-feeding species. The shape of their mouth, with top lip protruding over bottom lip, allows them to hoover their meals off the bottom. The pirk is simple enough to use; it is attached to the main line via a good quality swivel and then dropped over the side and allowed to sink to the bottom. Once it hits the bottom it is retrieved in two or three turns. The an-

Artiicial lures: hokkais and homemade pirks

A brace of cod

gler then begins the sink and draw movement by lifting the rod tip up in the air and dropping it again; this movement is continued until a cod is caught – it's as simple as that. A baited pirk will usually be more successful than an unbaited one.

White feathers are also pretty good for catching cod; these can easily be made up at home using a few turkey hackles tied on to a 4/0 or bigger stainless steel hook. When tying up traces for cod fishing, remember not to put more than two or at most three hooks per trace; cod are a shoal fish and three good cod on a trace at any one time will take some sort of miracle to get them to the surface. The flowing trace setup used to catch pollack will also prove very effective for catching cod, although heavier mono should be used on the flowing trace as cod will wear down the mono faster than a pollack would.

The above methods are among the best for catching cod, provided they are used in conjunction with large baits and large hooks and fished as close to the bottom as possible. And of course, the cod need to be there and playing ball.

Under current conditions you can spend many unrewarding days fishing for cod but don't let this put you off. If at first you don't succeed, try, try again. If you are lucky enough to catch a few cod, remember to take only as much home for the pot as you really need and release the rest. Any method of conservation put in place now by the angler, however insignificant it may seem at the time, may one day be the saviour of our sport.

TIP

Cod have bucket sized mouths so big baits are a must even for small codling.

Ling

8

A few years ago, at every competition I attended ling were a big part of the catch. You were almost guaranteed good catches of ling, but sadly this is no longer the case. Ling numbers, like cod, have plummeted; one of the main causes is believed to be the use of long lines by foreign fishing vessels in deep waters where the ling migrate every year to spawn, while ghost net fishing is another problem. Long lines used by these boats can carry up to 10,000 hooks per line, often stretching over hundreds of kilometres.

Ghost net fishing is even worse. These nets are discarded, lost or left for months at a time without being hauled, catching fish and shellfish indiscriminately. A survey and retrieval operation undertaken by Bord Iascaigh Mhara (BIM) in

Ling numbers have plummeted due to long lines and ghost net fishing

2005 lifted miles of monofilament nets that were ghost fishing, and some of the photos taken graphically illustrated the extent of the crisis. Immature ling caught by mistake on the long lines are dumped over the side of the boat; these will never get the chance to mature because ling react poorly to depth changes and when taken from even moderate depths will suffer from a greatly distended swim bladder which, in many instances, will protrude from their mouths. These immature ling are left struggling on the surface unable to return to the seabed, and will eventually be eaten by seagulls.

The ling has a long barbule under its chin

Ling (*Molva molva*) is one of the largest and hardest fighting members of the cod family. Although similar in size and shape, the ling is easily distinguishable from the conger. It is brighter in colour and has two dorsal fins; the first is short, while the second runs down its back to the wrist of its tail. The conger has only one continuous dorsal fin, which runs the whole length of its body. The ling has a long barbule under its chin, which is absent in the conger. This barbule is distinctive of the (*gadidae*) cod family. Ling, like congers, will grow to vast sizes; the Irish ling record stands at 55 pounds. but a specimen is any fish weighing 25 pounds or over. Like congers, ling are great lovers of wrecks and deep water reefs, but unlike congers they will hunt and kill their prey well above the bottom and have been caught as far up as mid-water. I have seen and caught ling on the top of shallow reefs while drifting using a flowing trace and a fresh sand eel.

For the sea angler, catching ling should be a fairly straightforward affair if he sticks to a few basic rules. These fish have a huge, fearsome mouth with an impressive set of dentures which it uses to catch and shred its prey, and for this reason the angler must use a large hook and equally large bait. Whole mackerel or large mackerel fillets seem to be the top bait for catching ling, but I have also had good results with herring, pouting, small pollack, coalies, sprats and large sand eels.

Use a large hook and equally large bait

Traces for catching ling are very basic; no need for flashy gear here. A simple pirk is one of the most effective pieces of tackle that I use and homemade pirks are every bit as good as the shop bought ones.

Making your own pirks

1. Buy a length of chrome-covered railing at any hardware shop.
2. Stand your piping vertically in a bucket of dry sand.
3. When the lead is melted pour it into the upright pipe and leave until it cools.
4. Mark the pipe at roughly the size you want your pirks to be (around 6 inches = 8 ounces) and then cut the pipe at 45-degree angles. The reason for the 45-degree angle is that it leaves it very easy to drill the holes for the split rings, which are needed to carry a hook at one end of the pirk and a swivel for the mainline on the other.

A short flowing trace of heavy mono or light wire about 4 feet in length with a spoon attached is also very effective. Those sonar type spoons are a big favourite of mine. I use the spoon about 6 inches up the line from a hook no smaller than a 6/0 offset hook that is sharp

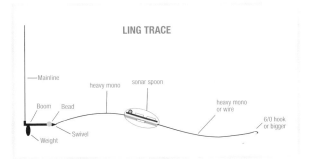

LING TRACE

Mainline
Boom   Bead
Weight   Swivel
heavy mono
sonar spoon
heavy mono or wire
6/0 hook or bigger

and of good quality. Hokkais also seem to catch more than their fair share of ling on a regular basis, but if you are planning to use them for a day's fishing

Sonar type spoons are great for catching ling

and ling are on the menu then I would advise you to tie them with a heavier mono than the standard type they are usually tied with.

Drifting over rough ground is the best method for catching ling ; you are more likely to come across some ling if you are covering a large area. Anchoring will also catch you ling but to a lesser extent than drifting, unless you find a wreck or reef that hasn't been fished in a while. While anchored you should use a conger trace instead of a ling trace, because you are sure to catch at least one conger and they are more

A ling struggles on the line (left)

A specimen ling

adept at biting through mono due to their strong jaws and their extremely sharp, close-set teeth. Although ling will take a bait as far up as mid-water, keep your bait as close to the bottom as you possibly can; this will greatly improve your chances of catching a fish. The bait needs to be changed every twenty minutes; a bait with no scent is no good unless you're lucky enough to land it on top of a very hungry fish. Ling are completely the opposite to congers in the way they take bait; large and small congers are cautious by nature and will only bite and mouth a bait very gently, sometimes taking several minutes before lifting and moving off with your trace. A good ling, on the other hand, could pull a rod over the side of the boat if it was left unattended. Their bite consists of a series of heavy pulls and most ling hook themselves by doing this. It is still advisable to strike with a sharp lift of the rod, just to make sure. If you don't catch a ling after you get a bite then the chances are that your bait is gone and you will have to reel in and re-bait your trace.

Ling, even small ones have a huge mouth of razor sharp teeth, so traces and hooks should be top quality and heavy duty.

Wrasse

9

T he ballan wrasse (*Labrus Bergylta*) has a large scaled body, a mouthful of extremely sharp teeth and a long spiny dorsal fin, which if rubbed from tail to head would leave your hand in need of bandages. The coloration of the ballan wrasse is extremely variable, from a deep brown to green to a freckled red. Little detailed work has been done on the growth or ageing of wrasse but one specimen of 16 inches was aged at twelve years. All ballan wrasse are born female, but after they mature a proportion of them change their sex and become male; this explains why most of the wrasse caught are females. Aquarium experiments have shown that wrasse spawn

Ballan wrasse congregates in colonies in rocky areas

between May and July. They form a nest lined with algae among the rocks, into which are laid tiny creamy white eggs which stick to the walls of the nest. Only wrasse over seven years of age are believed to be mature enough to spawn.

The best time of the year to fish for wrasse is from May until October, depending on the weather; if it has turned severely cold then the wrasse will have moved to deeper water. The Irish record at the moment for a ballan wrasse stands at just over 9 pounds and a specimen is 4.75 pounds or over, although most of the wrasse you catch will be between 1½ to 2 pounds.

Ballan wrasse & cuckoo wrasse   Cuckoo wrasse

The ballan wrasse is not a shoal fish, but it does congregate in colonies in rocky areas.

To fish ballan wrasse from a boat you will need to use rugged gear. Two hooks are more than enough to use when you are fishing wrasse, although nearly all your fish will be caught on the bottom hook. So for this reason it is worth baiting up your top hook with a piece of mackerel; this way you improve your chances of catching a cuckoo wrasse. You can catch cuckoo wrasse on marine worms but they seem to prefer a piece of mackerel or sand eel as bait. Your trace needs to be tied from mono with a breaking strain of not less than 20 pounds even though most of the fish you

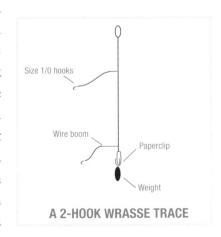

Size 1/0 hooks

Wire boom

Paperclip

Weight

A 2-HOOK WRASSE TRACE

will catch will only be around the 2 pound mark. The reason for using such a strong trace is because you will be fishing tight on the bottom and will, at some stage, get stuck in the kelp; most of the time it will pull out of the weed when it's tied with heavy mono, where lighter gear would be lost. Your two snoods coming out of the trace should have a few beads and a small spoon attached; the bottom snood is considerably longer than the top snood, so much so that when the trace is hanging out of the water the hook lies below the weight.

A small wire boom can also be attached to keep the bottom snood from tangling with the weight. More wrasse are caught on this type of trace than on any other that I have used. A handy tip for attaching the weight to the trace is by using a paper clip; this way if your weight sticks the paper clip will pull open and all you will lose is your weight. When fishing ballan wrasse please remember that all wrasse respond poorly to depth changes and when taken quickly from even moderate depths will often suffer from a greatly distended swim bladder. A slower retrieval rate once you get the wrasse clear of the bottom greatly increases its chances of survival when you return it to the water.

Your two snoods coming out of the trace should have a few beads and a small spoon attached

Ballan wrasse spend most of their day picking shellfish and marine worms off the rocks or hunting small crabs and shrimps through the weed and kelp, so for this reason your bait needs to be alive or as fresh as possible. The ballan wrasse will simply refuse stale or rotten bait. The best baits to use when fishing for ballan wrasse are marine worms or small crabs. Ragworms are the best of the marine worms to use, with lugworms coming in a pretty good second on most days. Small green hardback or peeler crabs are also excellent baits to use for catching wrasse. The hardback crabs should be around the size of a two-euro coin and when you are putting them on the hook they should be alive. Remove the second smallest leg from one side and put the hook in through the leg socket and out through the triangular shaped flap that covers their reproductive organs. If the crab is hooked this way it will stay alive longer on the hook and this will give your fish longer to locate the bait and will also make it more enticing for them. If you are using a peeler crab then a length of bait elastic is a good choice to keep your crab on the hook; large peelers should be halved before they are put on the hook. There is no need to remove the shells from your peeler crabs to fish for ballan wrasse; these fish have adapted to eating large amounts of shells as part of their diet.

Hardback crab

When you have your trace baited and ready for fishing let it go to the bottom at a nice steady rate. Once the line goes slack, put your reel in gear and retrieve it a few turns. You should not have to wait long until you get a bite; a wrasse bite is very distinctive – it consists of strong, quick pulls on the trace. When you feel this sort of a bite you need to strike very quickly and take a couple of quick turns on the reel handle to get the fish clear of the bottom. Once the fish is clear of the bottom you can take your time bringing it to the surface.

Always be careful when handling wrasse so as not to damage the fish or your hands, and always return as many of these slow-growing fish as possible.

TIP

If you are using hardback crabs, they should be around the size of a two-euro coin. Remove the second smallest leg from one side and put the hook in through the leg socket and out through the triangular shaped flap that covers their reproductive organs, the crab will live longer and be more enticing if hooked this way.

Coalfish

he coalfish (*Pollachius virens*) is often mistaken for its close cousin the pollack. But although similar in appearance, there are some distinct differences between the two. For example, the lateral line on coalfish is whitish in colour and fairly straight, while on pollack it is dark brown and curved. Another difference is in the mouth; the jaws of coalfish are level, whereas the bottom jaw on pollack protrudes well beyond the top jaw. Coloration is also different; the coalfish is darker on the back and whiter towards the belly than the pollack, which is generally brown on the back to a light brown towards the belly. In general, coalfish are darker in colour than their cousin, the pollack.

A brace of large coalfish

The coalfish is an active, gregarious fish, which can be caught in inshore and offshore waters at most times of the year. The Irish record for a coalfish is 33 pounds and the British record is over 37 pounds, but a specimen is any fish over 15 pounds in weight. Studies carried out on coalfish have shown that they have a maximum lifespan of twenty-five years and can attain a maximum weight of 70 pounds. The coalfish is known by several other names in many locations: saithe, glassan, and black jack to name but a few. Pound for pound the coalfish is a far more exciting and powerful fighter than the pollack.

Specimen coalfish

Large coalfish can be hard to find; smaller coalfish are easy enough to locate and can nearly always be found on the reefs where you would normally go fishing for pollack and ballan wrasse. But larger coalfish can turn up just about anywhere and when you're least expecting them; offshore wrecks are probably your best bet if you want to pick a fight with these truly powerful predators.

Speaking to workers at some of the fish factories where they were filleting herring, they told me that they often picked out several boxes of large coalfish and the occasional cod and pollack, which were mixed in through the herring. Some of these coalfish weighed in excess of 20 pounds. One particular coalfish weighed a staggering 23.5 pounds. These fish were obviously feeding on the herring at the time of their capture. Here is a great way of fishing for the really large coalfish; just find a shoal of herring, sprats or mackerel and try to fish below the shoal. Diving birds are a good indicator of where there's a shoal of fish. A live bait taken from the shoal would probably work best, or try a large chrome pirk with at least a size 4/0 hook and a whole or filleted fresh bait that you have just taken from the shoal.

Tackle for fishing coalfish needs to be around 15 pound class, the same type that you would use to fish for pollack. I personally like to use a 12 pound Shakespeare Ugly Stik original and a Penn GLS 25 lever drag. This outfit has proved itself to be successful on more than one occasion; the Ugly Stik rod has a very sensitive tip and the lever drag system on the Penn reels is one of the best systems in the world. A couple of years ago when I was fishing in a competition out of Bunbeg harbour in Co. Donegal we encountered a few large coalfish; at the time we were drifting over a reef for Pollack when they attacked our sandeels. Three rods on the boat bent over at the same time with the weight of three large fish. The line broke on the other two rods due to their star drag systems being set too tight and the unexpected attack by the coalfish. After several minutes and some seriously powerful runs I lifted a 12.5 pound coalfish into the boat. This would never have happened had I not had a good quality, lightly set lever drag system. After I landed my fish we went back to the top of the reef and tried another drift to see if we could catch some more of these fine fish, but sadly they were no longer there. In the space of

A full string of coalfish

those few minutes they had moved on in some other direction in search of food.

A lot of anglers that I know like to use some type of mono line for fishing pollack and coalfish, I find that there is too much give and take in mono compared to braid. The trace itself, which is tied up with around 12 feet of mono, should have just enough elasticity in it to stop the really big fish from breaking it or ripping the hook

Diving birds are a good indicator of where there is a shoal of fish.

Three up rig   Artificial eel

from its mouth. The hook you use should also be the same as that used for pollack; my personal favourite is a Kamazan B940 in a size 4/0 to 6/0.

A simple three up rig will catch the smaller to medium sized coalfish. At certain times you will catch the smaller fish three at a time until you get frustrated catching them and nothing else and all you want to do is move somewhere else. But to catch the larger coalfish you should only use a single hook rig; any more than one hook and you are going to lose the fish and the trace. I like to use a flowing trace, the same as I would use to catch pollack, with an artificial eel or worm of some kind. These can be fantastic for catching coalfish, especially over wrecks, but a freshly caught bait will be second to none. The top baits for catching coalfish are sprat, sand eels, herring and mackerel.

Coalfish are commercially fished, and provide excellent sport for the sea angler if they are fished for with light tackle. This will give them a chance to show their turn of speed as well as their powerful fighting capabilities.

A lightly set drag is essential if there is the possibility of large coalfish about; hokkais are excellent for catching small coalies.

Conger

11

The conger (*Conger conger*) is one of the largest fish that the sea angler is likely to encounter around our coastline. These extremely powerful and rugged fish have been known to grow to over 150 pounds, although most of these huge specimens have only been caught by commercial fishermen. The Irish record for a rod-caught conger stands at 72 pounds, while the British record is 133 pounds. A conger needs to be 40 pounds or over to make the specimen weight. Most of the conger that sea anglers will catch are called 'strap conger'. These are immature congers and are generally no heavier than 10 pounds; heavier fish are caught in between the 'straps' and the angler never knows if the next one will be a specimen. When I first began to fish for congers I was told by an older, more experienced angler that when an average conger was hooked and lifted clear from the bottom the fight would resemble holding the lead of a large dog which had just seen a cat. That statement was funny at the time but proved to be a

A conger needs to be 40 pounds or over to make the specimen weight.

pretty accurate description of a conger fight. It is almost impossible to over-estimate the strength of a very large conger ; there is no fish around our shores that is more capable of showing up a defect on your tackle than an enraged conger.

To fish for congers you need to use extremely strong tackle. Nothing under 50 pound class is of any use, and if you haven't got this type of gear then forget about fishing for congers. Rule No.1 when fishing for congers: never give a conger line once it has been hooked, because if it gets its tail wrapped around

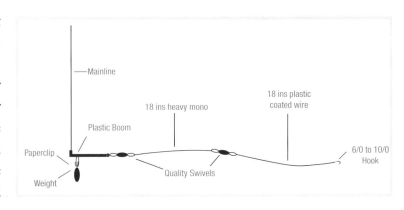

something there is no way of shifting it. Your trace from the hook needs to be about 18 inches of nylon-covered braided wire of 40-50 pound breaking strain to a good quality swivel, then another 18 inches of 50-60 pound breaking strain monofilament to another good quality swivel. On the mainline a small tube or sliding boom is needed to attach the weight. Then the mainline is tied to the top swivel on the trace. Remember to attach the weight to the boom via a paperclip or a light piece of line in case the weight snags on the bottom. Traces longer than 3 feet can be problematic; if the tide is running strong then a longer trace will allow the bait to lift off the bottom and when fishing for congers the bait needs to be tight on the bottom. One hook is more than enough when fishing for congers. I made a big mistake once while fishing in Killybegs; I was fishing my usual type of conger trace but instead of putting on a weight I attached a pirk, which is also very good for catching congers. But using a pirk and a trace together was in hindsight a bit silly. I hooked a good conger and had just got it off the bottom when a large pollack took the pirk and everything went crashing back to the reef. After a few minutes of pulling for a break the trace eventually snapped and all I was left with was a big pollack on my pirk.

Baits for conger seem to vary slightly from place to place, but as a general rule fresh mackerel or herring seem to be the top baits. Other baits include poor cod, pouting, coalies and grey gurnard. Studies carried out on the stomach contents of congers that were caught inshore showed that some 90 per cent of their diet consisted of three bearded rockling, poor cod and grey gurnard and the remaining 10 per cent were crustaceans (the swimming crab and the edible crab). Stomach contents of congers caught offshore showed that their diet consisted mainly of blue whiting, with a small percentage of argentines and squid showing up also.

To get the best results from conger fishing make sure that your baits are as fresh as possible; congers will sometimes take a stale bait but to a much lesser extent. Ground baiting while fishing is a good way of attracting more congers to the area you are anchored on, and a lot of skippers will put out a rubby dubby bag with the anchor.

When you have baited up and let your trace go to the bottom, leave your reel on the ratchet. That way if you are not pay-ing attention you will hear the first gentle bite, even though you may not have seen it. To strike at this stage would be a big mistake; congers will mouth their bait for a short time before they take it. My method of hooking a conger is as follows: after the ratchet clicks the first time I lift the rod gently and put the reel in free spool. These soft gentle bites can happen several times so I wait until the line starts to move; then I put the reel in gear and strike twice and take three or four turns on the reel handle to get the conger lifted off the bottom. The

Conger caught using mackerel

first few seconds are critical when you hook your conger. After you get it clear of the bottom the conger fights the whole way to the surface in a peculiar fashion, by shaking its head while swimming in the figure of eight before twisting up and down on the line as it nears the surface. Once the conger is on the surface the skipper should be able to gaff or net it to remove the hook and release the conger to fight another day. If you are fishing congers from a

Strap congers are excellent sport and you just never know when a monster conger will take your bait

dinghy, then you should have your t-bar on hand for when you get the conger alongside the boat and release the fish from outside the boat.

Do not take the conger inside the dinghy; once it is on the floor slithering about it can be all but impossible to lift it out again and you will end up sliding about on the slime along with the conger. Practise a catch and release policy on these rugged, hard-fighting creatures and protect our conger sport for the future.

TIP

Once you hook a conger, never ever give a it any line, because if it gets its tail wrapped around anything there is little chance of shifting it.

Haddock

12

As with a lot of our popular table species, the haddock was and still is under quite a lot of pressure from the commercial fishing sector. Our fishermen are hammered by quota restrictions and days at sea and are competing on a seriously sloped playing field with our European counterparts. Over the years, haddock has been over-fished to very low levels and a number of arrests of several foreign fishing vessels have revealed under-sized haddock catches in their holds; some of the haddock measured were less than six inches in length. Haddock this small are of no use for filleting for human consumption and will

Undersized haddock end up as fishmeal

only end up being used for fishmeal. Another reason behind the decline in haddock stocks, though to a lesser extent, has been the over-fishing of scallops. Scallops make up a large part of the haddock's shellfish diet, along with razor fish, which are probably also being over-fished at this time. In the last year or so there has been a slight improvement in reported haddock catches by anglers and fishermen alike. Perhaps some of the restrictions in force for the protection of this species are beginning to pay off, and maybe this could signal a return to the days when catching haddock on a day's angling was a regular occurrence.

The haddock (*Melanogrammus aeglefinus*) is a strong fighting member of the cod family (*Gadidae*) and there is a good resemblance between the two species. The haddock, however, can

be identified by its slightly forked tail, black lateral line and a dark spot on either side of its body, just below the lateral line and above the pectoral fin. This spot, as the tale goes, was caused by St Peter's thumb when he lifted the fish out of the sea. When a haddock is hooked and brought to the surface, its body is light purple in colour but this soon fades once it is on board the boat. The haddock is also credited

The haddock is a strong-fighting member of the cod family

with having better fighting qualities than the larger cod.

If given a chance the haddock has a life span of twenty years and can attain a maximum weight of 17 kilogrammes. The Irish record for a haddock stands at 10 pounds 13.5 ounces and the specimen weight is a fish of 7 pounds or over. But believe me, if you catch a fish of 4 pounds or over then you should feel more than delighted with yourself. The haddock's diet normally consists of scallops, razor fish, mussels, squid, cockles, shrimps, lugworms and soft crab. Fish baits will also work sometimes on their own or as part of a cocktail;sprat, mackerel and herring strips are the top fish baits. Mussels need to be tied on the hook with a few turns of some bait elastic. You can prepare your mussels in advance of a trip.

Preparing Mussels for bait

1. Push ten or twelve shelled mussels on to a piece of semi-stiff wire, then lace them well with bait elastic; when you're finished, all the mussels should slide off the wire in one thick worm-like length.

All the mussels should slide off the wire in one thick worm-like length

2. They can then be frozen in a length and cut to the desired size for the hook on the day of fishing; cocktails can also be made up using this method. Less fishing time is wasted for catching fish when your baits are pre-prepared.

If you know an area or you can get to a place where you have the possibility of catching a haddock, then the tactics for catching one are simple enough. Pound for pound the haddock makes the cod look very sedate in its fighting abilities, although haddock can tire very quickly if taken from the bottom at any speed. Over the past number of years, a few die-hard anglers and myself have had good catches of haddock while fishing out of Burtonport on a small patch of ground just off the Staag rocks. We normally encountered them while fishing over broken ground of sand, mud, gravel and shell. In the beginning we didn't go looking for them deliberately; instead, they found our bait. On such days, cod, whiting, pollack, cuckoo wrasse, pouting and gurnards were also partial to our bait.

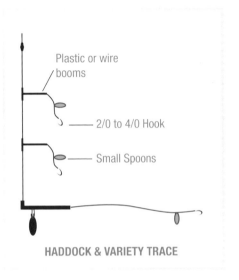

HADDOCK & VARIETY TRACE

All round traces need to be used for this kind of fishing. I usually use three hook traces that are strong but with small to medium sized hooks and some sort of attractors above the baits. I use small spoons crimped about two inches above the hook on long droppers, which are held away from the trace by small plastic or wire booms. I also leave the bottom dropper slightly longer than the top one; this acts like a mini flowing trace. Hooks should be of good quality and between a 2/0 and a 4/0 in size. Using hooks this size should cover most of the species you are likely to come across in case the haddock don't show up. Hokkais can also be brilliant for this kind of fishing; they are about the best all round trace that you can use for species fishing, but you must make sure they are of good quality, otherwise they will lose you more fish than they will catch. Baited hokkais will always out-fish unbaited ones; a good idea is to re-tie them with stronger and better quality mono than the original.

Hokkais are about the best all round trace that you can use for species fishing

Large haddock are much more cautious than smaller ones. Small haddock will attack a bait viciously and their takes will feel a bit like those of whiting, large haddock, however, have a habit of nibbling cautiously on your bait before taking it into its mouth. This is the reason why most big fish are lost through premature striking; the best method of hooking large haddock is to let them hook themselves. Because of the way it feeds, by sifting through sand and mud for its food, the haddock's mouth is much softer and smaller than that of the cod, so for this reason striking should be kept to a minimum.

If you are on known haddock ground and haddock are being caught, but you are losing fish because of striking too fast, then when you get your bait to the bottom take it up a couple of turns; you should then set your rod down against the rail of the boat securely but don't tie it, just watch and wait until the rod tip rattles and it will then bend over hard with a fish. This gives the haddock enough time to hook itself – then just lift the rod and set the hook into the fish. You will miss some other species of fish sometimes by not striking, but that's a small price to pay for a decent haddock. Always use a landing net to lift haddock into the boat safely; the hook will pull out of their mouths if you try to lift them in by the trace. Haddock can shoal in huge numbers so be prepared to move the boat in the same direction and at the same speed as the feeding haddock. The shoal moves constantly, combing the seabed for food.

A freshly caught haddock

Remember; when you are fishing haddock only keep what is absolutely necessary for your own needs. All too often, anglers have eyes bigger than their bellies and end up dumping part of their catch. Retrieve all your fish slowly; that way they can be released back to the water for another day's sport.

Whiting

13

Whiting (*Merlangius merlangus*) is another member of the cod (*Gadidae*) family. It is a highly sought after fish from a commercial point of view and, although not on the endangered species list yet, stocks are well depleted, like all other fish that are prized for the dinner table. These fish are delicious to eat and all too often when you're catching them you will feel the tendency to kill more than you will ever need.

It is up to each individual angler to adopt some form of conservation when catching whiting. There may be a lifeline for whiting in the not too distant future though; blue whiting, a close cousin of whiting, is becoming a prominent food source and seems to have the numbers to sustain commercial fishing for a while yet. Blue whiting is found at much greater depths than any other member of the cod family, as far down as 1,000 metres.

Blue whiting

There are also new quota restrictions coming in to force regarding most of the whitefish species.

The average weight of whiting that you will normally catch will be between 1 and 2 pounds ; the Irish record is 4 pounds 14.5 ounces, the British record is 6 pounds 12 ounces, while a specimen whiting is any fish over 3 pounds. Whiting has a life-span of ten years and after its first year it migrates from the safety of the shoreline to open waters. After commercial fishermen, the whiting's main predator is the cod. The coloration of whiting is quite variable, from a yellowish brown to a dark blue or green and often with a small dark blotch at the upper base of the pectoral fin. These fish are normally found at depths of between 30 and 100 metres over a bottom consisting mainly of mud and gravel but are occasionally found over sand and rocky bottoms. Whiting are caught all around the Irish coast and can be a very welcome catch on cold winter days when no other fish seem to be interested in the bait. They also venture very close inshore. Like cod, whiting is seen as a late autumn or early winter species, but sometimes when you are boat fishing on deep-water marks whiting can be caught during the summer months. If whiting could grow as large as cod they would be the number one target fish for the sea angler. They have a lightning turn of speed and a fantastic fighting ability that is lacking in the cod, which relies on its sheer weight and huge mouth as a defence against coming to the surface.

Whiting venture very close inshore

When fishing for whiting, most anglers will only bring worms as bait. Worms do catch whiting, but all you have to do is look at the whiting's tooth-filled mouth to know that this fish is a true predator. Any fish smaller than itself is going to be its prey, and marine worms are only part of its diet when food is not abundant. Chunks of oily fish can be particularly effective at catching whiting; long thin strips of squid and small sand eels will also work well.

The whiting's tooth-filled mouth

When average sized whiting are being caught on the boat at regular intervals, you can sometimes catch the bigger fish in the shoal if you are willing to take a gamble and try for them. When everyone else is catching their average sized whiting on three-up traces baited with worms and shellfish, I find that fishing a short flowing trace baited with a small whole sprat is great at consistently catching the larger whiting out of the shoal; sand eels and strips of squid will come in a modest second when you are fishing with the flowing trace.

The *Loinnir* fishing close to Arranmore lighthouse

The top baits for whiting are sprat, mackerel and herring strips, sand eels, shrimp, squid, razor fish, mussels, crabs, ragworm and lugworm.

Traces for whiting should consist of three hooks. The droppers on the trace should be about 6 inches long and each dropper should have some small attractors like beads or sequins attached. My own personal preference is to use small silver plastic spoons in between several brightly coloured beads; I find this trace more successful than any other for catching whiting. Mackerel feathers and hokkais also work very well, as do shrimp rigs, pink flasher lures and ordinary white feather traces like those you would use for catching cod, only with smaller hooks. Another trace that I use quite often is a variety trace that is tied in a similar way to that used for catching haddock. The bottom dropper is left much longer that the two droppers above and is held clear of the weight by a small boom. When the trace begins to fish on the bottom, this dropper acts as a mini flowing trace.

Hooks for catching whiting should be around a size 2/0, of good quality and extremely sharp; unlike the haddock, the whiting has a very hard mouth. The line above each hook should be checked for small cuts after each fish is unhooked; the sharp teeth of the whiting will destroy this mono over a period of time. Checking for the cuts can be done by simply pulling the mono between finger and thumb and feeling for the nicks. Once you come across

Bigger whiting are often caught on fish baits

teeth marks on the line the damaged piece of mono must be cut off and the hook re-tied; otherwise, the fish will eventually be lost with the hook still in its mouth.

Whiting should always be fished with as light a gear as possible; 12 pound to 15 pound class gear is more than enough for these fish. Even if you're catching whiting three at a time, they will still be unable to threaten your gear to any great extent. Always try and use as light a weight as possible and let the whiting show its true fighting ability.

TIP

When everyone else is catching their average sized whiting on three up traces baited with worms and shellfish, try fishing a short flowing trace baited with a small whole sprat, sand eels or strips of squid these will catch you the bigger whiting in the shoal.

Dogfish

14

There are several species of dogfish that can be caught around our coast at different times of the year. These include the lesser spotted dogfish, the greater spotted dogfish (bull huss), the spurdog and, to a lesser extent, the smooth hound and the starry smooth hound. Dogfish are members of the shark family and their skeleton consists of cartilage rather than bone. The lesser spotted dogfish (*Scyliorhinus canicula*) is known by several different names, including the small spotted cat shark, the rough hound and the doggie. For convenience, we will refer to it as the LSD within this chapter.

Specimen dogfish

The Irish record for LSD is 4 pounds 4 ounces and the British record is 4 pounds 15 ounces (the British record LSD was taken from the shore). A specimen is any fish over 3.25 pounds, but most fish will weigh around 2 to 2.5 pounds. Little is known about the biology of this fish but it is believed to be mature at 20 to 24 inches. It is extremely rare to hook immature LSDs; almost all those caught are adults. Each female lays between eighteen and twenty egg capsules that are attached to weeds by means of elongated tendrils. Egg capsules are laid in the spring and the young dogfish take from eight to ten months to hatch. The LSD is easily distinguished from its closest relative, the bull huss. It is much smaller in size than the huss, has smaller spots, and has one single nasal flap whereas the bull huss has two.

Bait for the crab and lobster fisheries

There was a time when LSDs would turn up at angling competitions in plague proportions but, sadly, commercial fishing and, to a lesser extent, pollution have badly affected their numbers. These fish are regularly targeted by commercial fishermen as bait for the crab and lobster fisheries as well as for the fertilizer and pet-food markets.

The LSD has an orange-brown back and a pale cream underside and has a vast array of small spots peppered over its back and sides. Its skin has a sandpaper-like texture (and was once used for scrubbing the decks of ships). When lifted into the boat the LSD will twist itself around anything it can, including an unwary hand as you try to unhook it, and its sandpaper-like skin will leave nasty abrasions on your skin which will take several weeks to clear up. If you catch one, hold it by the head and bring the tail up to meet it; this is the correct way to immobilize the fish so you can unhook it, and will in no way harm it.

Very few anglers enjoy fishing for LSDs, but they are often relied on to make up the catch numbers during sea-angling competitions. Once you catch an LSD you can be sure that there will be more to follow as they are a shoal fish. The LSD is an opportunistic feeder and will take fish, worms and all types of shellfish baits that are usually meant for other fish species. They are most active at night

When lifted into the boat the LSD will twist itself around anything

and will occasionally take a bait that is being fished well off the bottom. LSDs have poor eyesight and rely on their keen sense of smell to hunt for food.

LSDs are true scavengers, so when fishing for them, use stale bait; several-days-old mackerel is an excellent bait, as are frozen sand eels (for some unknown reason frozen sand eels are preferred to fresh ones). LSDs are normally found over sandy or muddy bottoms but are occasionally taken over rocky ground and reefs.

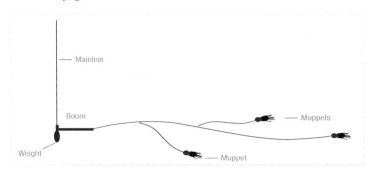

The gear required for fishing LSDs can be kept light unless you are fishing over or near a reef where there is a chance of catching something like a conger, ling or bull huss that will surely test your gear. If you are fishing on sand or mud then a 15 pound class rod or reel will more than suffice. I like to use this class of gear in case I hook a thornback ray that feeds in the same type of areas as the LSD. Traces for catching LSDs need to be tied from strong mono as these fish have small teeth which will prove to be very abrasive on the trace after a few are caught; always check above the hook for signs of wear on the mono. I like to have a three-hook trace flowing back behind the boom. A long trace up to 15 feet is recommended when the tide is slack and a short trace of 6 feet when the tide is running strong, I also like to incorporate at least one good quality swivel in the trace as well as the one at the boom. The hooks on the trace need to be of good quality; my personal preference is a 3/0 black Aberdeen B960, which is chemically sharpened and will penetrate through the fish's tough mouth with

Dogfish often break the surface curled up in a ball

TIP

When you feel the bite of an LSD, lift your rod tip and then let it down again. LSDs will pick up your bait, nudge it, chew it but take their time eating it, so if it looks like the bait is getting away from them they will readily gulp it, thus hooking themselves.

You can save time in competition fishing by lifting in two and three LSDs on your trace at a time

ease. These fish are not known for their fighting capabilities and will often break the surface curled up in a ball.

When fishing sea-angling competitions where fish numbers are being made up with LSDs, try the following:

When you feel the next bite do the same again. Once LSDs are hooked they lie where they are on the bottom and do not put up a struggle until they are lifted off the bottom. Try this technique – it does work, and you will save a lot of time if you are competition fishing by lifting in two and three LSDs on your trace at a time.

The LSD is probably the most resilient of any fish species that the sea angler will encounter, capable of living out of the water for long periods. Even when this fish is taken to the quayside for weighing purposes it can still be released afterwards. This fish should always be released alive and unharmed. Because of the serious stock depletions among so many other species, anglers are relying more and more on the humble LSD to make up the numbers during sea angling competitions.

Spurdog

The spurdog (*Squalus acanthias*) is closely related to the tope and shark families. It has the typical shark outline and body shape and gets its name from the two extremely sharp spines of bone (spurs) present on its back in front of its two dorsal fins. There is no anal fin present on this species. Unlike most members of the dogfish family, spurdogs do not confine their activities to the bottom alone; they are quite content to feed at any depth so long as there is an adequate food supply. Spurdogs are generally a deepwater species and may appear similar in outward appearance to juvenile tope. Its back and sides are a dreary brown-grey colour which sometimes can be peppered with small white spots. Its underside is cream to pale-white in colour. The body of the spurdog is long and slender and built for speed when hunting down its prey.

The average weight of rod-caught spurdog is usually around 7 pounds

The Irish record for spurdog is 21 pounds, 4 ounces, the British record is 21 pounds, 3 ounces and a specimen is any fish of 12 pounds or over. The average weight of rod-caught spurdog is usually around 7 pounds. The maximum reported size for spurdogs is 160 centimetres, and it can attain a weight of over 22 pounds. The growth rate of the spurdog is believed to be slow; it matures late, has a low reproductive capacity and is believed to be a long-lived species, with an estimated maximum age of up to 100 years.

Commercial fishing for spurdog in Ireland began off the Donegal coast and during the 1980s fishermen caught spurdog by the thousand in gill nets.

Boxes of spurdogs caught by commercial fishermen

Landings were almost 8,000 tons annually, but in the 1960s the North-east Atlantic fishery saw over 60,000 tons landed. Spurdogs were previously used in fertilizers, skinned and utilized for human consumption, but in the late 1980s the stocks came to near collapse due to commercial fishing pressures. The vulnerability of this species is evident. It is only in the last few years that spurdog numbers seem to have increased slightly.

The spines that give the spurdog its name can be a danger to the unwary angler. These spines can and do inflict nasty puncture wounds, which will usually require medical attention. When handling, the spurdog should be held by the wrist of the tail with one hand, with the other hand gripping it under the throat. Often during handling, especially during the months of August and October, female spurdogs that are caught will eject the young that they are carrying; these young are usually perfect replicas of the parent fish. Depending on the size of the female, it will carry between three to ten embryos and the gestation period takes almost two years. During August and October the females move closer inshore

Spurdog's spines inflict nasty puncture wounds which will require medical attention

to give birth to their young, after which they encounter the males and are impregnated on their journey back to the deep.

If located, spurdogs are very popular for the competition angler; they are shoal fish and once found the fishing can be frantic. Spurdogs are relentless killers and voracious feeders and have been called the hyenas of the sea. They are ruthless in their pursuit of prey fish; the shoal is sometimes given away by seagulls and gannets following them as they chase shoals of mackerel, sand eels and herring towards the surface, leaving a trail of blood and fish bits for the birds. Once a shoal of spurdogs moves into an area, other species already there are quick to vacate it.

A spurdog shoal is sometimes given away by seagulls and gannets

The gear required for catching spurdogs needs to be at least 20 pound class, especially if you are going to use more than one or two hooks. I like to use a 20 pound class rod and reel, but I will use no more than two hooks on the trace if there is the possibility of spurdogs in the area. I will fish 30 pound class gear with three hooks if I am going to fish spurdogs for numbers during a competition. Three spurdogs on a trace at any one time will seriously test the quality of your gear, and any faults from the hook to the reel will come to the forefront during the tussle.

Traces should be tied with heavy mono or wire. The spurdog's mouth contains a set of extremely sharp teeth, which they use to good effect for catching and ripping apart their prey. Traces tied of mono will also show the effects of the spurdog's teeth; just check the mono above the hook after you catch one. I like to use a short flowing trace rig around six feet in length with two hooks on it; in between the two hooks I like to put a good quality swivel. There is no need to use beads or spoons to attract this fish, as bait scent alone will see to that.

The hook you use is also very important; it must be top quality, strong and above all else extremely sharp to be able to penetrate the hard mouth of the spurdog. By now I am sure you know my preference in hooks. I only use Kamazan B940 in different sizes for all my fishing; a size 4/0 to 6/0 hook

Spurdogs must be handled with care

for spurdogs will work best. Baits for these voracious feeders can be just about anything, it really depends on what shoal of prey fish the spurdogs are hunting at the time you encounter them. If I was pushed for an answer on the top baits to use for spurdogs, it would have to be herring, mackerel, sand eel and sprat in that order; nine times out of ten, if there are spurdogs in the vicinity and you have one of these baits in the water then your chances are better than most of hooking one.

There is no way of deliberately targeting this species, as it spends its life roaming the ocean following its prey. Your best bet is to try an area where you see the gulls and gannets diving. If you do catch a spurdog, unhook it as quickly as possible, re-bait and get your trace back down among the shoal as fast as you can (.

Spurdogs are eaten in most parts of the world; I have tried them, but give me a fresh herring, turbot or dab any day. A catch and release system should always be used on this long-lived species.

TIP

For bait, steaks of herring or mackerel seem to work better than fillets; sand eel and sprat should be put on the hook intact.

Bull huss & smooth hounds

16

There are three other less common types of dogfish that are potential targets for the sea angler, namely the greater spotted dogfish (bull huss), the smooth hound and the starry smooth hound.

The greater spotted dogfish (*Scyliorhinus stellaris*) is commonly known as the bull huss or nurse hound. The bull huss is closely related to, but is easily differentiated from, the LSD (lesser spotted dogfish). It has two separate nasal flaps which are clear of its mouth and the anal fin extends to the middle of the second dorsal fin. Bull huss grow much larger than LSD and are reddish-brown in colour with larger spots and large dark

Bull huss or nurse hound

blotches. Both bull huss and LSD are targeted by commercial fishermen, sometimes for human consumption (sold as rock salmon), but are more commonly caught as bait for pot fishermen fishing whelks and, to a lesser extent, crab and lobster fishing. They are also caught and processed for fishmeal.

The bull huss can grow to 170 centimetres in length and can attain a weight of 25 pounds or more. The British record for a rod-caught bull huss is 22 pounds 4 ounces, the Irish record is 23 pounds 13 ounces, but a specimen is any fish of 16 pounds or over. The average size of rod-caught bull huss is between 8 and 12 pounds.

Unlike the LSD, the bull huss are 'loners'; they will normally lie in deeper offshore water over rough, rocky ground or around reefs. Known conger marks are also a good place to look for them and they are occasionally caught by rock anglers close to the shore. Bull huss are caught more successfully at night, although you will still catch some during daylight. Like their close cousins the LSD, they must be handled with extreme care because of their sandpaper-like skin, which will remove the unwary angler's forearm skin with ease.

Take extreme care because of their sandpaper-like skin

The number one bait for bull huss is without a doubt the sand eel. Other baits such as mackerel and herring, and even shellfish and marine worms, will attract them occasionally, but to specifically target bull huss I will always try sand eels first. Sometimes ragworm tipped with a fillet of sand eel will work very well.

Hooks for catching bull huss should be extremely sharp, in sizes 3/0 to 6/0. The rod and reel set-up that I like to use is a 30 pound class outfit. This may seem a bit on the heavy side for a fish that averages around 10 pounds, but remember that you are going to be fishing in deep water over reefs or rocky ground, which is also classic conger ground, so your gear must be able to handle them as well. Traces also need to be on the strong side. My personal preference is a leger rig, a small tubi-boom with the mainline running through it to a good quality swivel, then a length of 30 pound mono between 3 to 6 feet in length attached to another good quality swivel, and a small length of heavier mono or light wire between this swivel and the hook.

Once you are baited up, let your trace go to the bottom gently, and remember to let out enough slack line to keep the trace on the bottom. Whenever you feel a bite do not strike; leave the reel in free spool until the line starts to go out. Bull huss will play with the bait before swimming off with it while biting it, and once this happens you will need to strike two or three times firmly to make sure it's properly hooked. Bull huss have often come to the surface holding on to bait at the end of a trace, fighting all the way to the surface only to let go just before being netted.

The smooth hound (*Mustelus mustelus*) and the starry smooth hound (*Mustelus asterias*) look very much like small tope or sharks, although they do not have the same graceful shape as the tope; their fins are large in comparison with their body. Until recently, these two species were believed to be one and the same, with the starry smooth hound being thought of as just an immature smooth hound. The smooth hound is grey to light brown on its back, light grey on its sides and a creamy to pale white on the under side. the starry is the same except for a freckling of white spots (stars) on its back.

The smooth hound can grow to 5 feet in length and attain a weight of over 30 pounds, while the starry smooth hound is slightly smaller; the maximum weight is believed to be around 20 pounds. The British record for the smooth hound is 28 pounds, the Irish record is 16 pounds 8 ounces, and a specimen is any fish of 7 pounds or over. I cannot seem to find any definite recorded weights for the starry smooth hound.

A specimen bullhuss caught on a mackerel fillet

These 'hounds' give birth to live young much like the spurdog, with between 7 and 15 pups to a litter; the young are exact replicas of the adults. Both these species of 'hound' are pack hunters, so once you catch one you know that there will be more. Dawn and dusk are excellent times of the day for fishing these fish and they are without doubt the hardest fighters in the dogfish group.

Top baits are peeler crab and hermit crab, although they will occasionally take a fish, sand eel or worm bait as well as squid. Smooth hounds do not have teeth but have the same types of crushing plates as the ray family. These fish prefer a sandy, gravelly or muddy bottom; they are often found in estuaries and are caught close inshore during June, July and August. Hooks need to be good quality and a size

These fish prefer a sandy, gravelly or muddy bottom; they are often found in estuaries and are caught close inshore during June, July and August

4/0. The same trace that is used for the bull huss will also catch the smooth hounds, although there is no need to use wire above the hook to the swivel; ordinary mono will suffice.

A 20 pound class outfit is more than enough to catch these hard fighting fish. The smooth hound will play with your bait before taking it in its mouth so it is advisable to ignore first round bites. As with the bull huss, let the smooth hounds swim off with your bait before you strike. Make sure the drag on your reel is set correctly as these fish accelerate at incredible speeds once they realise that they are hooked and will put up a good struggle if caught with reasonably light gear. A lever-drag reel is probably the best type you can use for any of the harder fighting fish, as it is easier to reduce or increase pressure as required.

The smooth hound and the starry smooth hound are both over-exploited commercially for human consumption (the smell of ammonia that comes off them when they're dead is enough to put me off eating them) and for fish-meal. These fish have excellent fighting qualities for the sea angler and a catch and release method of conservation should be used when fishing them.

TIP

When you think you have a bullhuss at your bait strike two or three times firmly to make sure its properly hooked. Bullhuss have often come to the surface holding on to a bait at the end of a trace fighting all the way to the surface only to let go just before its netted.

Sharks

17

T here are several species of shark, offering sea anglers the possibility of a big game fish from Irish waters. The blue, porbeagle, thresher and mako are the main species, although the blue and, to a lesser extent, the porbeagle shark are the ones that the angler is most likely to encounter.

The porbeagle (*Lamna nasus*) is a cold water shark and spends most of the year around our coast. This is a heavy bodied shark with most of its bulk above its pectoral fins, making this a true big game species. The Irish record for the porbeagle shark is 365 pounds and the specimen weight is any fish over 150 pounds. The porbeagle can attain a weight of 500 pounds and live as long as thirty years.

Blue shark

It is normally encountered in deep trenches around rocky pinnacles and in the vicinity of shipwrecks, where there is a constant and plentiful supply of food.

The blue shark (*Prionace glauca*) prefers slightly warmer waters than the porbeagle shark and migrates into our waters during the summer months in pursuit of the large shoals of mackerel, herring and other pelagic species. The blue shark is a slender fish with large wing-like pectoral fins. It is dark blue dorsally and a vivid blue on both sides, which soon fades if the fish is out of the water for any period of time. The Irish record for the blue shark is 206 pounds, the British record is 218 pounds and a specimen is any fish weighing 100 pounds or over. Blue sharks are found worldwide and the current world record is a fish that was caught off the US weighing a massive 454 pounds. Their maximum age is reportedly twenty years. Unlike porbeagle sharks, blue

Charter boats get anglers to the shark grounds quickly

sharks are known to hunt in packs, so when one shark is caught there is a very good possibility of catching others. During lengthy spells of warm weather, the blue shark will occasionally chase its prey right onto the beach. Bathers watching this spectacle on the shore are often horrified, as it conjures up images from the film *Jaws*, which portrayed sharks in the worst possible light. Female sharks give birth to live pups and they are expelled from the female's body cavity once the pup's yolk sac is completely absorbed. Their gestation period lasts almost a year and each litter can consist of between 4 and 135 young sharks.

Boat angling for sharks usually commences in June and continues until October.

TIP

Commercial salmon fishermen are always a good source of information as they will let you know when the first sharks start to appear. Sharks often become entangled in their nets as they try to get a free meal by taking the ensnared salmon from the nets.

Before you start shark fishing the first and most important thing to do is to set up a scent trail to attract the sharks into your area; this is done by using a 'rubby-dubby' – a sack full of fish bits, pulped oily fish, bran and fish oil. The sack is placed in the water and tied alongside the boat so that the motion of the boat on the sea keeps the sack moving, giving off its precious scents and juices.

A specimen blue shark gets its photo taken before being released

A specimen blue shark is tagged and released

The gear needed for shark fishing is simple enough – a good 50 pound class rod and reel. The reel should be fully loaded with line or braid, whichever you prefer. The most important part of your equipment is your trace. Your shark trace should consist of a good quality hook in a size 8/0 to 12/0; this is then attached to a 250 pound wire trace with crimps and the trace should be about 12 feet long. There should be a good quality swivel in the middle of the trace as well as at the end of the trace to join it to the mainline. Some anglers prefer to attach a six-foot wire trace to a swivel, then attach six foot of heavy mono (at least 100 pounds) to a second swivel, which is then attached to the mainline. The swivel in the middle of the trace is designed to take out the line twist, as a hooked shark will spin the trace around its body on its way to the surface in a bid to free itself.

Freshly caught bait is essential for shark fishing ; mackerel are normally the number one bait. Fishing for fresh bait should continue while fishing for sharks as the movement of the struggling and distressed fish getting hooked will also add to the appeal for any sharks in the area. A freshly caught mackerel should be prepared into a flapper to use as the hook bait; remove

Blue sharks need to be handled with care while being lifted and unhooked

the backbone and the tail from the mackerel but leave the head attached.

Float fishing is the most productive method when fishing for sharks; the float can be set at any depth but if there are a few anglers or rods fishing then each float should be set at different depths. When a shark is caught at a pre-determined depth, the other floats can also be set at that depth to maximise your chances of catching more sharks. There is no need to let the floats and traces drift away too far from the boat as the rubby-dubby will attract the sharks right to the boat. The sharks will often attack the rubby-dubby bag as it hangs over the side of the boat, which also makes for an incredible and breathtaking scene.

Set your float at a pre-determined depth and then put your trace in the water. Let it drift away from the boat, about fifty yards should suffice. If a few rods are being used, set some close and some further away from the boat. Leave your rod in free spool but put the ratchet on. You may have to wait for hours to get a shark to take your bait but sometimes it only takes minutes; once a shark lifts your bait you will hear the click of the reel's ratchet speed up. Let the shark make its run and once the run has stopped engage the reel wind in any slack line and strike hard; the shark will make several more long runs before it can be brought to the boat. Always try to release your shark in the water as the numbers of these magnificent creatures are in decline. If it has to come on board let the skipper handle it; he will tail rope it and take it in safely.

Sharks are still targeted commercially, primarily for fins, meat and oil, and are often taken incidentally as a bycatch. One-third of European shark populations assessed are now considered threatened and another 20 per cent are at immediate risk of becoming so. Red-listed European sharks include spurdogs, porbeagle, basking, short fin mako, blue and several species of deepwater sharks. The lucrative global market for shark

Freshly caught bait is essential for shark fishing

fin, used for the Asian delicacy 'shark fin soup', is estimated to be increasing by 5 per cent each year and in 2003, the EU adopted a regulation prohibiting shark finning in EU waters and by EU vessels worldwide. But lenient enforcement standards means that it is still being carried out. Sharks are still being caught, their fins and tails removed and their carcasses dumped overboard.

If and when you get the opportunity to catch and land a shark, take a few quick pictures of your catch and then get it back into the water as fast as possible. Catching and releasing these fish is a sure way of guaranteeing sport for yourself and other anglers for the future.

Tope

18

T he tope (*Galeorhinus galeus*) is a small member of the shark family; it is an active and fast-swimming species and is found in marine waters from the surface to about 1,500 feet. The tope has a typical slender shark-like appearance with a long pointed snout, large pectoral fins and a large mouth with sharp triangular teeth. It has two dorsal fins, one large and one small, and five prominent gill slits on each side. Its large tail has a deeply notched upper lobe and the fish has a greyish, bronze to taupe coloured upper body and paler undersides.

The tope can grow to a length of 195 cm

The Irish record for a rod-caught tope is 66.5 pounds, the British record is 82.5 pounds and the world record is for a tope weighing 98.5 pounds, although a specimen is any tope over 40 pounds. The tope can grow to a length of 195 centimetres, attain a maximum weight of 45 kilogrammes and live as long as fifty-five years. The female tope gives birth to live young; the size of a litter depends on the size of the mother, bigger animals producing more pups than smaller ones, anywhere between six and fifty-two pups.

For many years, tope were considered a nuisance by commercial fishermen as these active hunters not only affected the boatman's livelihood by taking fish from their nets but also by becoming entangled in them, which resulted in many of the nets being totally destroyed. The species has sometimes been called the 'soup fin shark' because it is prized for its meat and its fins that, in the Far East, are made into shark fin soup. The tope is also exploited for its skin, which is made into beautiful leather, and its oil-rich liver, which yielded vitamin A before the discovery of the synthetic substitute. Populations of tope have been declining due to over fishing but it is still an important part of the catch in some places around the world. High mercury levels in the flesh has reduced human consumption and caused the collapse or restriction of fisheries.

Tope occasionally get caught in fishermen's nets

The tope has a well-merited reputation of being a true fighter; it is the most sporting of all the smaller sharks. The tope will put up a tremendous struggle when hooked on suitable tackle in shallow water, which allows the fish to show its true speed. The tope is one of the largest species encountered by the sea angler during the summer months.

Tactics for fishing tope are straightforward enough; these fish are bottom feeders so your trace needs to be on or very near the bottom. Successful tope fishing requires the boat being anchored on a known tope area over sand or a muddy bottom. A rubby-dubby bag can be put out with the anchor to help set up the scent trail. The rod required for tope fishing should be around 30 pound class, the reel also needs to be 30 pound class with a good drag system, preferably a lever drag which will allow you to apply and release pressure on the fighting fish with ease. Experienced anglers will occasionally fish with 20 pound class gear, but if you're a novice at this type of fishing then I would suggest you stick with the heavier option. The line on the reel should be braid or Dacron; monofilament line offers too much stretch, which can make it difficult to strike and maintain constant contact with the running fish.

Hooked into a good fish

Tope anglers rarely agree on the size of the hook and the length of the trace needed; some believe in long traces while others swear by short traces. The trace should consist of a good quality hook in a size 6/0 up to a 10/0, depending on the

A fine specimen tope

general size of fish in the area and the size of the bait being used. The hook should be attached to 6 feet of 100 pound wire and crimped securely; on the other end of the wire a good quality swivel should be attached and crimped, and on the opposite end of the swivel a 6 foot length of 100 pounds. Mono should be fastened and then attached to the swivel on the mainline, which is threaded through a running boom with a six or eight ounce lead attached. The reason for the two trace materials is that the wire guards against the tope biting through the trace and the heavy mono absorbs abrasion from the fish's extremely rough skin. There is no need for beads, attractors or lures on a tope trace; the only other thing that this trace requires to work successfully is fresh bait. In my opinion, whole mackerel is probably the best bait, with a flapper consisting of the head and two fillets attached and one with the tail and backbone removed coming in a close second.

When you have baited up, let your trace over the side of the boat until it hits the bottom; do not re-engage the reel but put the ratchet on. Now a waiting game begins. There are times you might have to wait all day or even several days before you get a tope run on your gear; then again, you might only have to wait a few minutes. Sometimes something as simple as a change in wind direction or the turn of the tide could see several runs occurring at the same time on the boat. Typically, when the tope picks up your bait it may begin the run quite slowly but then quickly gathers speed. To strike at this point would be disastrous and would surely lose you your fish, as the tope will only be carrying your bait in its mouth. Once the run slows

A standard tope trace

then it's time to strike; there is no need to strike more than once. After the strike, everything usually goes slack; this is normal. Once the tope feels the hook it usually changes direction and swims at full speed towards the boat. Now the angler must reel in as much slack line as quickly as possible before the tope gets the chance to go under the boat and cut the line on the keel. The battle between angler and fish can go on for a half hour or more depending on the size and quality of the fish. There is nothing more exhilarating for an angler than seeing a large tope coming to the side of the boat with his trace in the corner of its mouth.

Remember to take a few quick pictures of your prize fish and return it to the water as fast as possible so that it can live to fight another day. Sadly, tope numbers, like a lot of other species, are in decline. Thankfully, however, most anglers now practise a catch and release on these fish, which will help increase numbers in the future.

TIP

If you want to have a serious chance of catching a tope then you really need to go to Rathmullan in Co. Donegal. This is without a doubt the best tope area in the country and the angling club will advise you on how and where to best catch them.

Rays

19

Blonde Ray

The blonde ray (*Raja brachyura*) is the largest of the ray family and can easily grow to over 40 pounds in weight. The Irish record stands at 37 pounds and a specimen is 25 pounds or over. It is light brown in colour, has a few lighter blotches with a heavy scattering of dark spots all the way to its tail and to the tips of each wing and its underside is creamy white. The blonde ray is slightly less angular than its cousin the thornback ray but does not possess the razor sharp thorns that are the characteristic trait of the thornback. Blonde rays are caught at the same locations using the same methods, tactics and baits as described later for catching thornback rays.

Blonde ray (*Raja brachyura*)

Thornback Ray

The thornback ray (*Raja clavata*) is the most common ray found around the Irish coast. It is highly prized and sought after by sea anglers and commercial fishermen alike as a valuable table fish. As its name implies, it has a number of thorny spines on its back and tail and it is these razor sharp spines that must be avoided while handling the fish. Tip: Regular thornback anglers usually carry a piece of towelling for holding on to the ray until they can safely remove their hook. The thornback ray has a diamond shaped body with two dorsal fins almost at the tip of the tail. The tail itself is ringed with a distinctive black banding and the underside of its body is a creamy white colour. The thornback ray has many colour variations, but is usually a greyish-brown colour overlaid with pale or dark spots surrounded by smaller darker spots. Cuckoo ray, homelyn ray and blonde ray are often confused with the thornback ray because of these different colour variations, but the sharp thorns on its back is the best way of identifying it from all the others. The thornback ray can attain a weight of over 40 pounds. The Irish record stands at 37 pounds and the British record is 31 pounds 7 ounces. A specimen is any fish that weighs 20 pounds or over, although the majority of the fish that you are likely to catch will usually weigh no more than 10 pounds.

Thornback ray (*Raja clavata*)

Thornback rays are associated with a seabed consisting of sand, mud or gravel, but occasionally they are caught over kelp or rock marks, which are surrounded by a sandy or muddy bottom. A tidal race with a sand bank at the mouth of an estuary or, even in the estuary itself, are among the most common places where the angler is likely to come across these fish. Thornback rays have been caught in water depths ranging from 150 fathoms to as little as 4 feet. The thornback ray is responsible for the egg cases known as 'mermaids purses' which are often found along the shoreline. They are more likely to be caught in shallower waters from May right throughout the summer months as they feed on a variety of fish, shellfish and marine worms which frequent the shallow waters during the summer months; this is why they are classed as a summer species for sea angling. Catches indicate that thornback rays usually travel in small groups consisting of several males and only one female, which is normally the biggest fish in the

The thornback ray has many colour variations

Where there is a tidal race with a sand bank, at the mouth of an estuary or even in the estuary are among the most common places where the angler is likely to come across these fish.

group. The female tends to be given first refusal on any food that the group comes across and this is usually the reason why the first ray taken on a boat is a female fish.

Once one ray is caught the rest of the group are usually caught in quick succession, so unhook your fish as quickly and as safely as you can, re-bait and get your trace back to the fishing zone as fast as you can. Beware of the thornback's mouth when removing your hook; this fish does not have sharp pointed teeth, but instead has flat abrasive crushing pads. The jaw muscles are very powerful and will crush the unsuspecting finger if it goes in the mouth, leaving you in a great deal of pain.

Thornback rays are true scavengers and will pick up just about anything edible off the seabed. Most successful anglers who fish regularly for thornbacks will swear by baits which are sometimes several days old and stink beyond belief. If they only have fresh bait then it's left out in the sun until they

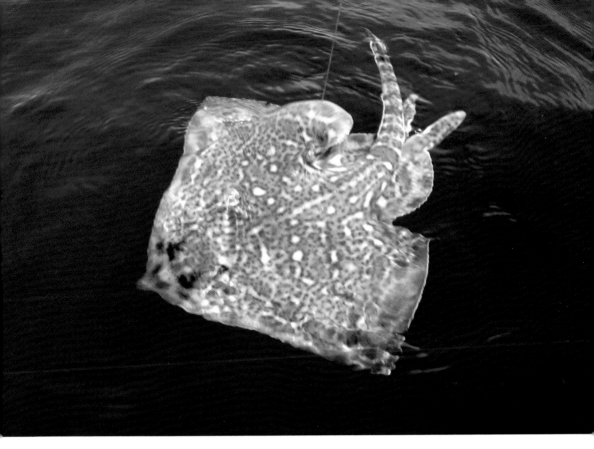

Most successful anglers who fish regularly for thornbacks will swear by baits which are sometimes several days old and stink beyond belief

are ready to use it, but fresh bait will still occasionally catch rays.

The top baits for catching thornback ray are mackerel, herring, sprat, sand eels, shrimp, razor fish, peeler crab, hermit crab, ragworm, lugworm and squid. As you can see from this selection of baits, the thornback ray will eat just about anything. My personal favourites are mackerel, sand eels and razor fish and sometimes a cocktail of any of these. I always use a flowing trace rig with just one hook for thornback ray fishing; if the tide is running hard I use a short trace of about 4 feet and if the tide is slack I will use a long trace up to 12 feet and sometimes more. I use a swivel on my trace about a foot above the hook and between the hook and swivel I use heavy mono of 20 pounds or more to combat the abrasive pads in the thornback's mouth. The hooks I use for fishing thornbacks are the hooks I use for most of my fishing, Kamazan B940's in a size 4/0. They are extremely sharp and strong, two factors that are required for catching thornback rays. Do not under any circumstances put a used Kamazan hook back in with unused Kamazan hooks or it will rust the whole batch overnight.

The boat needs to be anchored for fishing rays, and once your weight and trace hits the bottom, enough line needs to be let out to make sure that your

bait stays there. At times the thornback ray can be felt pouncing on top of your bait; it then begins to manoeuvre over the bait until it can catch it with its mouth. This is the same technique that rays use to catch their prey when it is alive. Time must be given for the thornback ray to take the bait in its mouth before you strike, as striking too soon means you will either hook the ray through one of its wings (if your hook's sharp enough) or lose it altogether. Thorn-

A thornback ray

back rays are not known for their fighting abilities, but they use their body size and the tide to their advantage and will kite in the water, which will sometimes make the angler think that the fish is bigger than it really is. There is some evidence of a decline in catches of these fish so any that are not required for the table should be returned alive.

TIP

Because thornback rays are a shoal fish, once one is caught the rest of the group are usually caught in quick succession, so un-hook your fish as quickly and as safely as you can, re-bait and get your trace back to the fishing zone as fast as possible.

Gurnards

20

There are six different species of gurnard associated with the Irish coast, although only three of these, the grey gurnard, red gurnard and tub gurnard, are caught on a regular basis by the sea angler. There is also limited commercial fishing of the three species.

Gurnards are widely distributed around the Irish coast over all types of seabed. Their odd triangular appearance is due to their large bony head, which is devoid of either skin or scales. Their body is short and thin and tapers quickly towards the forked tail. Armaments in the shape of short, sharp spines are present around the head, gill covers and dorsal fins. They are predominantly bottom-feeding fish, and the lower three rays of the pectoral fins are separated into long finger-like tactile sensors, which are used to move the gurnard along the bottom as well as hunt-

A good tub gurnard

ing out its prey on the seabed. By using the separated rays as props the gurnard can gain an advantageous view of the surrounding area.

With the help of special muscles which vibrate the swim bladder, they can produce a dull growling sound. The term 'gurnard' comes from the French word *grouger*, which means, 'to grunt'. Several gurnards on the deck at a time can make a strange chorus of sounds. Great care must be taken when handling gurnards as these fish have numerous sharp spines, which can inflict painful cuts and stab wounds, although these spines are not actually poisonous. Lifting the gurnard by its under-belly will help keep your hands clear of its spines.

Grey Gurnard

The grey gurnard (*Eutrigla gurnardus*) is the most common species of gurnard to be found around the Irish coast. It can be found anywhere from the

shallows to a depth of 75 fathoms. It is a long-lived fish and has been known to reach a maximum age of seventeen years. The Irish record for grey gurnard is 3 pounds 1 ounce and the specimen weight is a fish of 1.5 pounds or over. Grey gurnard are commonly found over sandy ground and are often caught on rigs meant for plaice or dabs. Fishing for grey gurnards is a relatively straightforward affair. The area to be fished should have a sandy bottom and you

Grey gurnard (*Eutrigla gurnardus*)

can anchor or drift; either way it should not take them too long to find your bait. Gear for fishing grey gurnards should be the same as that used for fishing dabs and plaice – a 12 pound to 15 pound class rod and reel is more than adequate. Traces should be tied up with 15 pound to 20 pound mono, a simple one up and two down rig with small spoons and a few bright colourful beads above 1/0 or 2/0 good quality hooks. You must fish your trace as tight to the bottom as you possibly can. The best baits to use for grey gurnard are sand eels, razor fish, mackerel, herring, sprat, peeler crab, ragworm and lugworm and they are also partial to a piece of fresh gurnard meat. It is not unusual to catch two or even three grey gurnards at a time.

Red Gurnard

The red gurnard (*Aspitrigla cuculus*) is also a very common species of gurnard for the sea angler. This fish is almost tropical-looking with its bright red colour, and is found all along the eastern Atlantic and throughout the Mediterranean at depths between 15 to 100 fathoms. It is also a long-lived gurnard and can reach a maximum age of twenty-one years. The Irish record for a

Red gurnard (*Aspitrigla cuculus*)

red gurnard is 3 pounds 9.5 ounces and the specimen weight is a fish of 2 pounds or over. Several red gurnard have been caught by commercial fishermen weighing over 5 pounds. In addition to sandy areas, red gurnard also inhabit broken and rocky sea beds. Probably the best all round trace to use for red gurnard is a two up and one down rig. The two hooks above the weighted boom should be on snoods at least 6 inches long with small spoons and several brightly coloured beads. Tip: I like to leave the third/bottom snood at least 18 inches long so that it can flow enticingly in the tide, and about 4 inches above the hook I like to attach one of those mackerel spinners which are red on one side and silver on the other, and shaped so they spin with the currents in the water. For some reason this trace out-fishes all the others that I have tried for red gurnard. The hooks used should be of good quality, chemically sharpened (to get a good hook hold in its hard mouth) and in sizes 1/0 to 4/0. I sometimes like to use a 4/0 if there's the possibility of a few codling in the area. The best baits for red gurnard are sand eels, strips of mackerel, herring, sprat and razor fish. You will regularly catch more than one red gurnard at a time, but the bigger gurnards will usually be on the bottom/third snood with the spinner. Hokkais also work well for this species.

Tub Gurnard

The tub gurnard (*Trigla lucerna*) is the largest member of the gurnard family. It is not as common as the grey or red gurnard, but what it lacks in numbers it makes up for in weight. The Irish record

Tub gurnard (*Trigla lucerna*)

for the tub gurnard stands at 12 pounds 3.5 ounces, but a specimen is a fish weighing 5 pounds or over. It is believed that the tub gurnard can attain a maximum weight of 15 pounds. These fish mainly inhabit areas of sand or broken ground. Their lifespan of fourteen years is shorter than that of the grey or red gurnard. Like the red gurnard, the tub gurnard has almost a tropical look to it with its bright red colour. There is confusion at times between tub gurnard and large red gurnard; however, the tub has a vivid bright blue border to the tip of the large pectoral fins, which is missing from that of the red gurnard. The same type of traces used to catch red gurnard will also work well for tub. This is a strong active fish and when caught and brought close to the

surface it can occasionally be seen jumping several feet out of the water in a bid to free itself from the hook. The tub gurnard's diet consists mainly of fish. The best baits to use are sand eels, mackerel strips, small sprats, poor cod, pouting, small plaice, small dabs and strips of fresh gurnard. When baitfish is plentiful, tub gurnard will rise off the bottom and actively feed with bass and mackerel.

A colourful tub gurnard

It is difficult to fish for tub gurnard specifically; they are usually caught as a bonus while fishing for red gurnard.

There are three other species in the gurnard family, namely lantern, piper and streaked. These gurnards usually prefer deeper waters but occasionally a streaked gurnard, which is also bright red in colour, gets caught and it is often confused with a tub or red gurnard. The streaked gurnard has a blunt shape to its head and the vertical streaks on the flanks are unmistakable.

Remember that these are long-lived fish, so a catch and release system should be practised when fishing them. Take a camera with you on a day's fishing so you can take a picture of the gurnard and then release it alive.

TIP

I like to leave the bottom snood on my trace at least 18 inches long so that it can flow enticingly in the tide and about 4 inches above the hook I like to attach one of those mackerel spinners which are red on one side and silver on the other – it is shaped like this so it spins with the currents in the water.

Turbot

21

The turbot (*Scophthalmus maximus*) is a left-handed fish – that is, a fish with both eyes and colouring on its left side. These fish are a real prize catch for any sea angler lucky enough to encounter one. Commercial fishermen extensively hunt turbot to such an extent that they are now a rare catch for most sea anglers. The decline of turbot stocks and the demand for turbot as a table fish means they command a high price in fish markets. Over the last number of years there has been some success in farming turbot; farmed turbot could in the future help ease some of the pressure on the wild stock.

The turbot can grow to over 55 pounds in weight and have a lifespan of twenty years. The Irish record for a rod-caught turbot stands at 34 pounds and the British record is 33 pounds 12 ounces, but any fish of 18 pounds or over is a specimen. Very few anglers will be lucky enough to catch specimen size turbot; most fish caught will be a lot smaller.

Turbot (*Scophthalmus maximus*)

The turbot's coloration can be quite variable from one area to the next but its back is normally a greyish-brown with a thick freckling of darker spots and blotches. The surface of its back is covered with hard bony tubercles, which makes it feel very rough to the touch. The lateral line curves around the pectoral fin then straightens to the tail. Owing to its large size, the turbot is difficult to confuse with other members of the flatfish family, but occasionally a large brill can be confused with the turbot, although the brill is less oval in shape and its skin is smooth

The turbot's coloration can be quite variable from one area to the next but its back is normally a greyish-brown with a thick freckling of darker spots and blotches.

to the touch.

The turbot is a nomadic fish. It lives on a seabed consisting mainly of sand where there is a strong run of tide or currents, on or near a sandbank. These fish have a unique ability to blend in with the surrounding colours of the seabed and when hunting, their camouflaged skin and their being partially buried in the sand makes them almost invisible to their prey. Small fish and sand eels, which are the main diet of the turbot, sometimes get caught in the tide and are swept over the edge of the bank where the turbot are normally waiting to catch them for a handy meal. Turbot are known to occasionally leave the bottom to catch their prey, and recent evidence suggests that during the hours of darkness they actively feed off the bottom. Turbot are classed as a summer species, but sometimes during the winter, cod fishermen returning from a day's fishing on an offshore bank will have the bonus of a turbot among their catch.

The gear required for fishing turbot needs to be relatively heavy, no lighter than a 20 pound class rod and reel. This is because you will need to use relatively heavy weights in the strong tides to be able to keep your bait on the bottom.

Getting the right amount of weight on your line is important. When the boat has settled at anchor you want your trace to begin fishing from directly below you on the seabed, and then slowly, with the correct amount of weight, be able to let your trace work its way back in the tide, working back along the seabed by lifting the tip of the rod; this is called trotting.

By lifting the rod you are lifting the weight off the bottom and this allows the tide to catch the weight and trace and carry it a few feet along the bottom; too much weight and the trace will stay directly below you, too little weight and the trace will be too far off the bottom. Line must also be let out for this method to work successfully. Working the trace in this way allows you to cover a large area of the seabed without having to shift the boat. As a rule, turbot generally lie partially covered for their prey to come within striking distance.

A simple one-hook flowing trace tied with at least 8 inches to 1 foot of 40 pound mono above the hook to a good quality swivel is required. The reason for this short length of heavy mono is because the turbot has a mouthful of extremely sharp teeth which would easily cut through light mono long before it could be taken to the surface. At the other end of the swivel 20

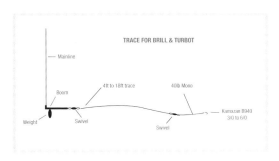

pound mono will be enough. The overall length of the trace can be anything from 4 feet to 20 feet. I prefer to use around 8 feet if there is a strong run of tide and around 15 feet if the tide is slack.

There is no need to bring a vast array of baits with you when you go for a day's turbot fishing, sand eels are the number one bait but I have also had some success with small whole sprats, while a belly strip of mackerel will

Turbot's camouflaged skin makes them almost invisible to their prey.

also work well. If you can possibly get and keep your sand eels alive, then you are in with a better chance of catching turbot than most – turbot will almost always attack a live distressed sand eel before a dead one. If you are fishing a live sand eel, you must only hook it through the bottom of its mouth; if you hook it through the top and the bottom of its mouth it will not be able to filter water and will die very quickly. Sometimes a fillet of a large sand eel will also work very well if it is only hooked on lightly and allowed to flutter in the tide.

Turbot do not waste any time taking food; they have relatively large mouths and extremely sharp teeth so their bites will be a series of strong pulls on your line. Like most flatfish, turbot use the currents and flow of the tide to their advantage when hooked, making them feel a lot heavier than they really are and testing your gear to its limit.

The sight of a nice plump turbot breaking the surface of the water is something that will always stick in the memory of the serious turbot angler. Let's hope it's a view that others will get to see for many years to come.

Brill

22

Brill (*Scophthalmus rhombus*) is another left-handed fish with both eyes and colouring on its left side. Like its close relative the turbot, this fish is a real winner for any angler who catches one. Highly prized as a table fish, brill is keenly sought by commercial fishermen.

Brill can attain a weight of 18 pounds. The British record for a rod-caught brill is 16 pounds and the Irish record is 9 pounds 8 ounces. A specimen is any fish weighing 5 pounds or over, although most brill caught by sea anglers will rarely exceed 3 pounds. The brill is simi-lar looking but smaller in size than the turbot; large brill are often mistaken for medium-sized turbot. The body of a brill is less angu-lar, thinner and more slender in shape, and its skin is smooth to the touch, compared to that of the turbot. Its upper dorsal fin extends right down over its eyes. The brill's coloration can vary greatly from one area to the next; it has the ability to change the colour of its skin

Brill (*Scophthalmus rhombus*)

on the eyed side of its body to match the surrounding bottom on which it is resting. Generally the back of the brill is greyish-brown to olive green with a heavy freckling of dark spots and whitish patches.

Not a lot of people know that flatfish are not born flat; for the first few weeks of their lives they are like any other fish. Then a process called metamorphosis begins, when the fish develops into a flat shape and the left eye moves around to the other side of its head.

The best time for catching brill is between May and October. Strong

Strong currents in the vicinity of sandbanks is where you are most likely to find these fish.

currents in the vicinity of sandbanks is where you are most likely to find these fish. Any area that is known for turbot will also have brill; an area of sand at the edge of a rocky outcrop (often indicated by the presence of fishermen's creels) is a good area to try. Brill are rarely fished for deliberately and most are caught by anglers who are fishing for turbot or plaice. Brill prey on small fish, sand eels and prawns. In strong tides some of its prey will find it diffi-

cult to hold its place on the sandbank and will end up getting swept over the edge; this is why brill and turbot lie in wait on the down-tide edge of the sandbank. Brill have a much more active lifestyle and move about the bottom far more than turbot do. They are often caught on baits that are meant for plaice, and they will take lugworm or ragworm on a regular basis. If a dead bait is going to be used it should be as fresh as possible because brill are not

An area of sand at the edge of a rocky outcrop is often indicated by fishermen's creels

scavengers and will rarely take a stale bait.

Live sand eels are fantastic for catching brill and you may also get the opportunity to catch a turbot on a sand eel. Live prawns are also excellent bait for catching brill and the occasional plaice; these can be easily sourced from fishermen if you cannot get your own.

The gear used for fishing brill has got to be the same as that for fishing turbot because of the possibility of catching the latter. Therefore, at least a 20 pound class rod and reel is required. The trace used for fishing brill is the same as that used for fishing turbot – a flowing trace with a single hook tied with a short length of at least 40 pound mono to a good quality swivel. Like the turbot, the brill has an impressive set of extremely sharp teeth which would cut through light mono with ease. On the other end of the swivel, a length of 20 pound mono back to the boom will suffice; the length of the trace can be anything from four feet up to eighteen or even twenty feet. I prefer to use a trace of about 15 feet long. The weight you use should just be able to hold

At least a 20 pound class rod and reel is required to catch brill.

bottom so that you can trot your trace back with the tide. A good quality hook should be used when fishing turbot and brill. I like to use a Kamazan B940 in sizes between 3/0 and 6/0 depending on the size of bait you are using and the size of fish that are usually caught in the area.

If you use a Kamazan B940 or any chemically sharpened hook, throw it away after your day's fishing is over; it will only rust and weaken if kept for a second day.

Another method which can be used to catch turbot and brill if the conditions are right is to drift for them. To fish on the drift your trace is still the same as the anchored method except you must use a weight, which will keep your trace tight on the bottom. When you feel your lead tap the bottom do not re-engage your reel. Hold your rod at all times, keeping the reel in free spool and checking the flow of line with your thumb. Once your lead touches the bottom release an extra 20 or 25 yards of line, then as the boat drifts over the bank periodically raise and lower the rod tip to re-confirm your trace is still on the bottom; if not, release more line. After a couple of drifts your lead should be bright and shiny from being dragged over the sand; this will verify that your trace is fishing correctly. At the first indication of a bite you should release the pressure off the line for about thirty seconds so that the trace

Live shrimps can easily be sourced from shrimp fishermen

and bait are stationary on the bottom, giving the fish a chance to take the bait properly and ensuring a good hook up.

The top baits for brill are sand eels, ragworm, lugworm, shrimp, razor fish and strips of mackerel. When fishing for brill you may also catch dab, floun-der, plaice, lesser spotted dogfish, thornback ray and, if your luck is in, a nice turbot.

TIP

Brill will eagerly take worms, especially lugworms, so it is worth hooking a lugworm or two above the sand eel when fish-ing for turbot and brill.

Plaice

laice (*Pleuronectes platessa*) is a right-handed fish and is widely distributed around our coastline. It is the most sought after flatfish in our waters because of its desirability as a table fish. It has a powerful oval body with bright orange to light red spots. Its eyes and coloured half are on the right side of its body and like most fish its colours vary slightly from one area to the next. The underside of the plaice is white with a chevron pattern. Apart from some bony tubercles behind the eyes, the scales are so small and so well embedded in the skin that it feels very smooth to the touch.

The British record for a rod-caught plaice is 10 pounds 4 ounces, the Irish record is 8 pounds 4 ounces, but any fish of 4 pounds or over is a specimen. Sadly, plaice of 4 pounds and over are becoming extremely difficult to catch; fewer and fewer specimens are caught each year due to over-fishing by commercial trawlers, so enjoy it when you catch a nice one. Studies carried out on plaice have reported that these fish can live as long as fifty years

Plaice (*Pleuronectes platessa*)

and can weigh in excess of 12 pounds. Spawning takes place from January until April or May; at this time they eat very little. Plaice may undergo quite prolonged spawning migrations; it has been calculated that, by using the midwater currents and only periodically settling on the bottom to rest, an adult plaice may cover 18 to 30 kilometres per day.

Plaice is a species that is associated with the summer months for the sea angler, although these fish are often caught close to the shore in late September and October and in the late springtime, if the weather is mild. The best times for fishing plaice are those hot calm sunny days that we sometimes get in July and August; on days like those there is no need to even anchor the boat. A slow drift can be more productive on these mirror calm days; plaice are an inquisitive fish so a slow drift will give the trace enough movement to attract the fish to the hook as well as allowing your gear to

Plaice is associated with the summer months for the sea angler

cover more ground. One thing to remember when you are fishing for plaice and for most types of flatfish for that matter: never strike too quickly. When you feel a bite make sure that you have enough line going out if the boat is drifting slightly; this way you can ensure that the bait is not being dragged away from a potential prize fish.

Unfortunately, extensive inshore trawling has ruined many of the best plaice grounds. Your best chance of catching a large plaice will be on small sheltered marks that boats cannot reach and where there are mussel beds close by.

There are a number of different traces that can be used for fishing plaice; my personal favourite, and one which can easily be used by the beginner, is the double spreader. This trace consists of a length of stainless steel wire with a small loop at either end for attaching the snoods and in the centre of the wire is a swivelled clip, which is looped at the top for attaching it to the mainline and a clip at the bottom for attaching the weight. Double spreaders come in various

Fishing for plaice

lengths, from six inches to two feet; a lot of anglers that I know make their own double spreaders for a fraction of the price of a shop bought one. Snoods can be of any length, usually somewhere between 6 inches and 2 feet and on each snood I like to attach several brightly coloured beads and a small silver spoon, and finish off with a good quality long shanked Kamazan B940 hook from a size 2 up to a 2/0.

A flowing trace with three hooks and a sonar spoon a few inches above the last hook works well

The only reason I would use a 2/0 hook is if there is a possibility of catching something larger like a lesser-spotted dogfish or a thornback ray, as these fish would straighten or break a size 2 hook.

TIP

I sometimes attach a snood above the double spreader; this hook will attract any fish that is not lying on the bottom, and I have caught grey gurnards, dabs and the occasional plaice on this higher hook. A flowing trace with three hooks also works well and I like to use a sonar spoon a few inches above the last hook.

Top baits for plaice vary slightly from one area to the next, but as a general rule mussels are the top bait followed by razor fish, ragworm, lugworm and shrimp. Other types of shellfish such as scallops, clams, cockles and limpets will also catch plaice but to a lesser extent. When mussels are being used they must be tied securely on the hook with bait elastic to stop the plaice from removing them before getting hooked. I like to prepare the mussels that I am going to use in advance of a day's fishing; this method of preparing the mussels was explained earlier in the section on haddock.

A different bait on each hook will show you what the fish are interested in when you start your day's fishing, but do not change all your baits to one type until you are sure that this is what they are feeding on. A cocktail of the baits

Burtonport, Co. Donegal

mentioned will occasionally out-fish an individual bait, while a bait tipped off with a small piece of squid or a small sand eel can also work well. According to most literature on fishing, sand eels are not renowned for catching plaice but in Burtonport plaice have been caught on small sand eels on more than one occasion. Give them a try; if the plaice show no interest you will always catch dabs, rays, dogs, grey gurnards and, if you are very fortunate, a nice brill or turbot.

Remember, when fishing for plaice fish with as light a tackle as you possibly can; these fish are not tremendous fighters but you will get some sport in fishing them with light gear as well as having something nice to look forward to for dinner.

Plaice has a powerful oval body with bright orange to light red spots

Sole and Dab

24

Sole

Sole (*Solea solea*), as its name suggests, is the shape of a shoe sole; it is also known as the black sole and the Dover sole. The sole is a nocturnal flatfish and is vigorously sought after as a highly prized table fish by sea anglers and commercial fishermen alike. Its skin feels like sandpaper to the touch and is a dark greyish-brown to reddish-brown with darker blotched markings on the body, while the mouth is hook shaped. The Irish record is 6 pounds 5 ounces and the British record is 6 pounds 8 ounces, but any fish of 2 pounds or over is considered a specimen. The sole can grow to around 7 pounds in weight and may live as long as twenty years. The sole is not directly related to any other flatfish species; it is the only true sole. There is another flatfish called a lemon sole, but it is not a true sole; it is a member of the right eye flounder family

Sole: a nocturnal feeding flattie

along with plaice, dab, flounder and halibut. The sole usually lives in sandy or muddy bottoms into which it burrows to hide itself and search for food. This fish is known as a summer species as it will retreat to deeper waters during the winter months when food becomes scarce.

This nocturnal feeding flattie lives on a diet of molluscs, worms and crustaceans. Rragworm and lugworm are the top baits but small strips of razor fish also work well at certain times. Occasionally the sole is caught during

daylight hours, but these are usually very dull days with the water heavily coloured, thus stopping all the light from reaching the bottom.

Fishing for sole offers a whole new experience in sea angling; fishing at sea in the dark can feel pretty daunting to all but the most experienced night anglers. Safety must be a priority, so if you are planning a night of sole fishing make sure your skipper is highly experienced and up to the task and make sure the boat is carrying all required safety equipment before you depart.

Tackle for fishing sole should be light

Tackle for fishing sole should be light; 12 pound class rods and spinning reels are all you will need. Traces should be about 6 feet long with three droppers and fished off a lightly weighted boom. I like to add a small spoon and a few beads on each dropper above a good quality size 4 hook. This hook may seem very small to use for sea angling, but the sole has a very small mouth and if you use a hook that is much bigger you will miss a lot of fish.

Once the skipper anchors the boat over renowned sole fishing grounds, put your trace over the side and let it go slowly to the bottom so it does not tangle before it hits the seabed. Once the trace hits the bottom make sure you let out enough line to keep it there. There are times when sole will be caught two at a time, depending on the area being fished and if there is much competition for food on the seabed.

Dab (*Limanda limanda*)

Dab

The dab (*Limanda limanda*) is one of the smallest flatfish species that the sea angler is likely to catch. The Irish record stands at 2 pounds 5.5 ounces and the British record is 2 pounds 12 ounces but a specimen is any fish weighing 1.5 pounds or over. Some commercially caught dab have been weighed at over

3 pounds. The dab is easily recognisable by rubbing its skin from tail to head. The skin can be light brown to dark brown in colour and feels very rough to the touch because the scales are ctenoid (spiny) on the upper surface.

All flatfish species are either right handed or left handed; i.e. the eyes are both to the right of the mouth making them left-handed or to the left of the mouth making them right-handed. Turbot, brill and megrim are left-handed fish while plaice, dab, sole, flounder and the huge halibut are all right-handed.

The dab will sometimes be a serious nuisance when you are fishing for plaice; your bait is no sooner on the bottom when you see the rod tip rattle with the weight of another dab on the hook. Then there are occasions when the dab will become the backbone of a day's fishing on the sand, when nothing else is interested in your bait. There are times when there

The skin can be light brown to dark brown in colour and feels very rough to the touch because the scales are ctenoid (spiny) on the upper surface.

seems to be no end to the number of dabs beneath the anchored boat that are eagerly awaiting to take the bait; sometimes when using three hooks on your rig you will catch three dab at a time. There is serious competition between dab for any food they find; once one fish is seen feeding, the other dab in the area move in to try and get a piece of the action.

TIP

When you feel a dab hooked on your trace, don't be in too much of a hurry reeling it in; sometimes if you wait a minute or two you will often catch a second dab and occasionally a third.

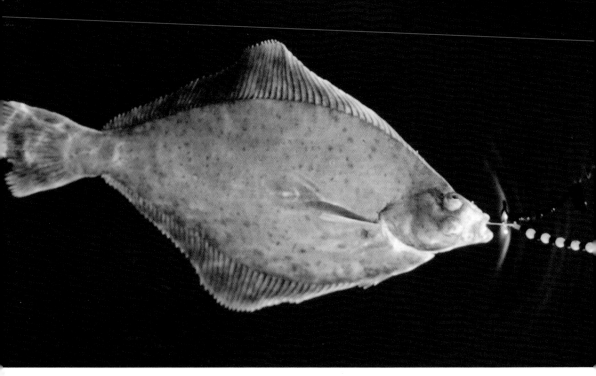

Dab is underrated as a table fish

The top baits for dabs are lugworm, ragworm, crabs, shrimps, mussels, razor fish and small pieces of fish or sand eel strips. Stale worms seem to work better than fresh ones and I have had several successful days fishing dab with leftover frozen ragworm. The same gear used for fishing sole should also be used for fishing dab; even if you are catching them three at a time they will not put any real pressure on light gear. Traces for dab are also the same, but the size of the hook can be increased to a size 1 or a 1/0, as a dab's mouth is a good deal wider than that of sole.

Dab, in my view, is very underrated as a table fish; I find it almost as tasty as plaice, and sole is absolutely delicious to eat.

BAITS

Baits required for all fishing

Preparation of baits and tackle before you go to sea is very important and usually starts several days before the outing is due to commence. Bait is not essential for catching all species of fish – pollack, coalfish and the occasional cod will take lures when no baits are available. Bait in some form added to your hook will definitely increase your chances of catching, and going fishing for a day without some is taking a bit of a  gamble. Lots of anglers catch and collect their own bait; this not only cuts down on costs but also gives you a certain satisfaction when you catch a fish on bait you have collected yourself.

There are many different types of bait that can be used for sea fishing – and almost anything caught in the sea can be used as bait. Some baits are excellent in certain areas, while others will not work there but will be effective in other areas; the reason for this is that fish like to eat the type of food they are used to. For example, you might catch fish using crab or shrimp over a mussel bed but if you use mussel on your hook then nine times out of ten your catch rate will greatly increase.

Mackerel

25

T he number one all round bait, the most popular and generally the most easily accessible of all is mackerel. Mackerel (*Scomber scombrus*) is one of the easiest fish to catch and the most prolific around our coasts during the summer months. These fish are the perfect target species when introducing novice anglers to the sport of sea angling. The Irish record for a rod-caught mackerel is 4 pounds 2 ounces and a specimen is any fish over 2.5 pounds. Anglers fishing with feathers will catch mackerel three, four or five at a time when the fish are in feeding mode. Spinning with a small red and silver spinner on a light rod is excellent sport, as is fly fishing with a single bright fly shaped like a small sand eel.

Mackerel (*Scomber scombrus*)

The mackerel is streamlined and hydrodynamically shaped for lightning bursts of speed as it attacks its prey and avoids becoming prey itself. Its body, apart from its head, is covered with minute scales and tapers to a delicate but extremely powerful forked tail; it has a big mouth with numerous small sharp teeth.

The most striking thing that you will notice about the mackerel is its magnificent markings; its back is covered with dark stripes intermingled with iridescent blue and green ones, the coloured flanks are also iridescent and the belly is a silvery white. This colouring provides the mackerel with exceptional camouflage which help it avoid bigger predators such as dolphins and tunas. This species also has another unique way of evading predators; as it has no swim-bladder it has the ability to dive rapidly to the seabed and then return to the surface layers just as quickly.

Mackerel are a very oily bait that few fish will refuse and can be used in different forms as bait for almost every species of fish when fishing from both boat and shore; even freshwater anglers use mackerel for pike fishing. Predatory fish as well as commercial fishermen hunt mackerel relentlessly and, on the face of it at least, their stocks still seem pretty strong for the future. Mackerel can be bought in most fish shops in season or vacuum packed and frozen from tackle shops all year round. At the start of boat angling trips time is usually spent searching for fresh mackerel. This is important, especially if conger or sharks are your targets, as stale or even day-old mackerel are no use as bait for these species.

Mackerel are not rated as a sporting catch, but can you imagine the sport that anglers could have with them if they could grow to 10 or 15 pounds in weight. During mid and late summer huge shoals of mackerel can be found all around the coast close to the shore, and they can be seen chasing small sand eels onto beaches and around piers. Small spinners and light spinning gear will give you excellent sport while spinning from harbour walls or rocky outcrops.

Mackerel are often chased to the surface by dolphins and sharks

At sea, a good indicator of a shoal of mackerel is birds diving on the surface; these birds are usually snapping up the sand eels or baitfish that the mackerel have chased to the surface, and the mackerel themselves are often chased to the surface by dolphins and sharks. Mackerel usually snap at any type of lure that you put down but traces with brightly coloured feathers, fluorescent beads and silver tinsel usually work the best. These traces should have no more than three or four hooks, any more than this and you will waste a lot of the allotted time untangling your trace. As you catch your mackerel you should store them out of sunlight immediately, preferably in a cool box, as once they have died the mackerel's flesh starts to break down and decay very quickly. Mackerel should be stored on ice if they are to be taken home for the table or for freezing for another day's fishing.

Day old mackerel, mackerel left out in the sun or even frozen mackerel work better than fresh mackerel when fishing for thornback ray and dogfish.

How to prepare a mackerel as bait

To prepare a mackerel for a day's fishing is easy enough. There are really only two ways of preparing it: filleting it or turning it into a flapper. The latter is the preferred choice for tope, conger and shark fishing.

1. Filleting mackerel needs to be done with a sharp knife; a blunt knife will only tear at the soft flesh.
2. Place the fish on a flat, even surface
3. Cut into it just behind the small fin at the back of the gills.
4. Run the blade along the backbone until you reach the tail, keeping the blade flat along the backbone as you fillet. This procedure allows you to remove the fillet in one piece.
5. Now turn the fish over and do exactly the same on the other side;
6. You should now have two nice fillets for bait.
7. Once you get used to filleting there will be very little flesh left on the carcass. The fillets can then be cut into whatever size pieces you want to use depending on the fish to be targeted, or the fillet can be used whole for bigger species. The head and back bone can be kept for a rubby-dubby bag if one is being used.

Making a flapper out of a mackerel is slightly more difficult but with a bit of practice can be done quite quickly. Again on a flat even surface start to fillet at the tail and work the knife along the backbone up to the gills before turning the fish over and doing the same on the other side. But once you reach

Filleting a mackerel

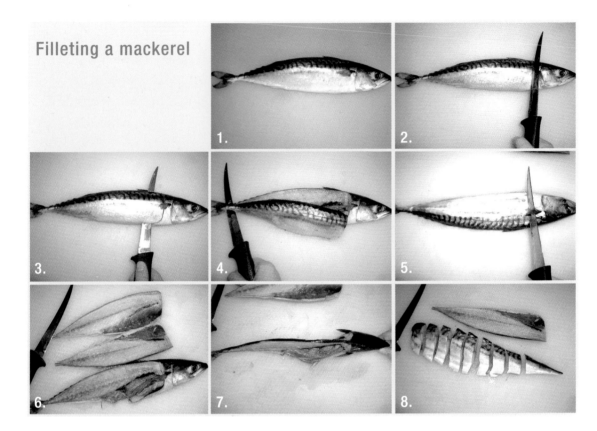

1. 2. 3. 4. 5. 6. 7. 8.

the gill this time cut through the backbone and remove it. You now have one flapper prepared for conger, tope or shark fishing. Four to six mackerel should be more than enough for a general day's sea angling unless they are small joey mackerel, although a lot more bait is required for tope, conger and shark fishing.

Herring, sprat and scad are also good oily fish to use for bait, although they are not always available and are an unusual catch for the sea angler. The scad can be filleted and used in the same way as mackerel, the herring can be cut into steaks, and the sprat can be used whole.

TIP

Mackerel should be stored out of direct sunlight immediately, preferably in a cool box. Once dead their flesh starts to break down and decay very quickly. Mackerel should be packed in ice if they are to be taken home.

Sand Eels

26

Another popular bait, and one which some sea anglers pay a small fortune for over the year, is the sand eel. These insignificant looking small fish are not eels at all but marine fish that sustain a highly commercial fishery in EU waters. They are caught and then ground up and used in the manufacture of fishmeal and fish oil, which has a variety of uses but mainly in the production of animal feeds for livestock, poultry and farmed fish.

In recent years, the sand eel fishery has attracted a good deal of controversy; with catches varying between 600,000 tonnes to 1 million tonnes per year, it has been questioned whether such a large fishery is sustainable and if it is causing ecological damage. Some fishermen and anglers believe that the over-fishing of sand eels is a major factor in the depletion and indeed the collapse of some fish stocks, notably cod, haddock and turbot.

Overfishing of sand eels is causing ecological damage

In European waters there are five species of sand eel. The two main species fished are the small sand eel, which grows to around 20 centimetres in length, and the greater sand eel, the 'launce', which can grow to about 40 centimetres in length. The two species are commonly associated with each other and catches of sand eels usually contain both. Sand eels vary greatly in colour; they can be a light sandy colour to a deep green across the back. The tip of the pectoral fin reaches as far as the front end of the dorsal fin. A dark spot

Inshore sand eels can be seen in tight dense shoals inside most estuaries and also frequent the low water tide line of shallow surf beaches

is located on each side of the snout and the lower jaw protrudes out beyond the upper jaw. Inshore sand eels can be seen in tight dense shoals inside most estuaries and also frequent the low water tide line of shallow surf beaches and the numerous banks and gullies associated with sand bars. Sand eels protect themselves by burying quickly into sandbanks and gravel and remain buried at night, coming out to feed at dawn. From October to March, however, they remain buried during the day in a dormant condition. During the winter their energy requirements are very low and they live off fat accumulated during the summer. The larger sand eel, otherwise known as the 'launce', prefers the habitat provided by sunken wrecks, although they generally inhabit the mid water to upper reaches by day, only dropping back to the seabed by night to bury into the sand. Pollack, coalfish, cod and turbot close to the wrecks target these fish in large numbers.

Any high rising sandbanks or reef lying offshore will also have its resident population of sand eels.

Collecting Sand eels

Inshore sand eels are generally raked. This is done with a small, thin, curved knife-like tool known as a 'vingler' drawn through the upper layers of sand along the angled edges of inshore sandbanks. The best banks to try are those that sit next to pools of standing water or slow running channels. Sand eels prefer wet sand, so stay low on the bank. Ask some of the older locals what beaches are known to have sand eels; you could be lucky enough and find yourself on a beach that no other sand eel collector knows about.

Collect sand eels with a vingler

1. Draw the 'vingler' repeatedly towards you in short strokes and about 3 to 4 inches deep in the sand, no more.
2. The blade should cut through the sand easily until a sand eel gets trapped in the curve. You will know when you have an eel trapped, as there is a definite resistance, which can be felt with the vingler.
3. Lift the blade upwards rapidly and be ready to grab the sand eel on sight as it emerges from the sand.
4. Alternatively you can develop a technique which consists of pulling the sand eel out of the sand and flicking it into your bucket; this takes some getting used to but will prove to be a faster method in the long run.
5. Be prepared to lose a lot of sand eels, as they are difficult to hold on to and are ultra quick!
6. Beware: while raking, the poisonous lesser

Draw the 'vingler' repeatedly towards you in short strokes

When you feel resistance there is an eel trapped

weaver fish adopts the same burying habit in the same ground as the sand eel and can leave you in excruciating pain and in need of medical attention if stung.

Having a constant supply of sand eels is every sea angler's wish and being able to collect your own is a dream come true, but I do not know where you can acquire a vingler or if there is such a thing for sale. A good friend made mine for me and I can tell you now that the value of my vingler to me is priceless.

Sea gull fishing for sand eels

Fishing for sand eels

When afloat inside estuaries it is possible to hook sand eels on float tackle using tiny size 18 hooks and minute pieces of mackerel flesh. Shoals are easily spotted by sea gulls diving on them. Another tip that works well on occasions is to tie a small bloody butcher or teal, blue and silver trout fly on light line about 6 to 8 inches behind a silver spinner; the sand eel follows the spinner and then attacks the fly. The larger offshore sand eel or 'launce' will eagerly take mackerel feathers or hokkai lures at times, although most end up getting foul hooked. But, by changing these feathers or lures for much smaller ones on size 6 or 8 hooks, the launce can be legitimately hooked in the mouth. Silver is the best colour of all, and sometimes they will even bite small undressed nickel-plated hooks. Small lengths of white or red silicone tubing over nickel-plated hooks will also work well on occasion.

Live storage

Sand eels require a constant supply of oxygen and frequent changes of water if they are to be kept alive for angling. Anglers can keep the eels alive in a plastic bucket linked up to a small portable aerator or alternatively submerged in a bucket with lots of small holes. If you're using an aerator try to have it running constantly; keep the eels cool and away from direct sunlight. When travelling to and from your particular fishing venue the constant shifting of the water inside the bucket can sometimes be enough to add sufficient oxygen without an aerator. Do not overcrowd the bucket; about twelve or fifteen average sized eels to a gallon of water is more than enough. Keep checking for, and removing, any dead eels; for some reason one dead eel seems to kill off the others very quickly.

Freeze about fifteen or twenty eels to a bag

Frozen sand eels are excellent bait and often prove better than fresh dead ones. Work out roughly how many sand eels you need each time you go fishing and place this amount in individual bags, I freeze about fifteen or twenty eels to a bag. Sand eels should be frozen as quickly as possible; once dead they decompose very quickly. While en route to your fishing venue use a cool box with plenty of ice packs or wrap the sand eels frozen in multiple sheets of newspaper or layers of polystyrene for insulation. Another good method for transportation of frozen sand eels is a wide thermos flask; sand eels will stay frozen for about 6 hours in one of these, even during a scorching summer's day.

Using Sand Eels for Bait

Sand eels will catch just about anything, from pollack, bass, codling, coalfish, mackerel, ray and turbot to bull huss, tope, dogfish, wrasse, flounder, plaice, brill and whiting; just about any hungry fish will take a bite at a sand eel. Most lures are designed and used to mimic sand eels. The rig you use will depend on the target species and the area being fished. The most common use for sand eel is to put it on a 4/0 hook at the end of a 6 to 15 foot flowing trace for pollack, coalfish, bass or any other predatory fish, while it can also be used in pieces on two up or three up rigs for any of the smaller species or as fillets on bottom traces for small flatfish. When drifting for turbot in deeper

A shoal of sand eels

water the backbone should be removed from the larger launce leaving the fillets attached to the head, as you would when preparing a normal mackerel flapper bait. The actual hook point in the sand eel is always best positioned towards the head in large sand eels as predatory fish eat sand eels headfirst. If you are going to use live sand eel for bass or pollack, use only enough lead weight to get the eel down to the fish. The more lead you use, the less natural the eel will appear to the fish.

TIP

When storing sand eels alive, do not overcrowd the bucket, about twelve or fifteen average sized eels to a gallon of water are more than enough. Keep checking for, and removing any dead eels. For some reason one dead eel seems to kill off the others very quickly.

Crabs and Ragworms

T hese next baits are not as regularly used by sea anglers, primarily because of the difficulty in obtaining them at certain times, but they are equally successful at catching fish. Peeler crabs, velvet crabs, hermit crabs, ragworms, mussels, clams, razor fish, cockles, limpets, periwinkles and shrimps can on occasion be collected along the shoreline and in rock pools at low tide. These so called lesser baits will often help you catch great fish when the more popular baits are not available or when you have run out. Almost any sea creature can be used as bait; even small versions of the species you are fishing will be taken by the bigger fish. Any extra bait that you manage to collect should be prepared as best as possible and then frozen for those days when you don't get a chance to collect any.

Peeler crab

Peeler crabs

Although not as frequently used as mackerel, sand eels or lugworms, peeler crabs and ragworm are popular baits with sea anglers in certain regions and probably should not be included with these other 'lesser' baits. Peeler crabs are commonly used for certain species, especially some of the flatfish, but unless you can collect your own peelers, getting enough for a day's fishing can put quite a hole in your pocket. Peeler crabs can be found in old tins, under stones, in cracks on seaweed-covered rocks or under any old junk along the low tide mark. Old tyres can be left along the shoreline in out of sight places; crabs that are ready to peel always look for a place to hide from predators while they shed their shells, and they see the dark insides of the old tyres as the perfect location for this. The ideal time to collect the crabs is just before they moult, although soft crabs that have just moulted still make good bait. When you are ready to use the peeler crabs as bait, first break off the legs and claws; then peel the shell off the body, put your hook through where its legs were and feed it out through the other end. Once on the hook the crab should be secured by a sufficient amount of bait elastic as the crab will not stay on the hook as it descends towards the seabed or if cast out. The individual legs can be used for tipping off the soft bait, and large crabs can be halved before being put on the hook. Small hard-backed crabs are used differently, and the legs do not have to be removed (see the section on wrasse for details).

Ragworm

Ragworm

King ragworm is probably the best marine worm you can use, possibly even better than lugworm. One advantage the ragworm has over the lugworm is movement – and lots of it. When the ragworm is slightly hooked through its head or tail it moves through the water like a snake, and the bites you get from predatory fish as a result of this movement are astounding. King ragworm are collected in only a few locations around the Irish coast. Buying them for as much as €15 a pound in some places is the only option for many sea anglers and it is for this reason that lugworm are more popular. The smaller harbour ragworm is more common and is also excellent bait; it is found in many estuaries and inlets around the coast. All ragworms are difficult to store and after a day or so they begin to break each other up. Broken ragworm bits are okay for dab or ballan wrasse or for use in cocktail baits, but are of little use for catching most other species. Early season pollack love big wriggly ragworm, which they attack with gusto. At this time they are best used on a long flowing trace with very little weight so as not to restrict their snake-like movement through the water.

Lugworm

28

Another favourite of the sea angler is the lugworm, an extremely common marine worm that can be found in sandy muddy areas all around the Irish and British coasts. If you live anywhere near the coast you are sure to know a hot spot for digging for them.

Types of Lugworm

Lugworms are large marine worms that live in U-shaped burrows in the sand or sand and mud mixes. Their presence on a beach or mudflat is given away by the piles or 'squiggles' of sand deposited above the burrows. The more squiggles, the more worms. There are two types of lugworm that the sea angler is likely to come across – the black lug and the blow lug. These species are common around most of the Irish coast. The cast, which is the coil of defecated material lying on the sand surface, and frequently seen at low tide, can usually be used to identify the species. Black lug usually has a neat, round coiled cast, often

Lugworms

like a Catherine wheel, while the blow lug cast is a bit of a mess. Black lug are usually found lower down the inter-tidal area, sometimes only visible on the larger spring low tides, while blow lug are found in greater numbers higher up the beach, and can often be observed on the smallest neap tides at low water.

Identification

The black lug is the larger species of the two, with an average size of between 20 and 30 centimetres, while the common blow lugworm grows to a maximum of 20 centimetres. The larger worms are found in the richer marine habitats farther down the beach. Worms vary in colour at different times of the year, anything from jet black to purple, brown, red or even pink. Blow lugworm have very soft bodies, with a hard 'tail' that is filled with sand. Black

The cast piled high in spirals, is a sign of fresh worm activity

lugworm are bigger and tougher and are the preferred lugworm bait of experienced sea anglers. They are only collectable at low water, when the water is farthest from the shore. The lugworm lives in a U-shaped burrow and there is a depression above its head at the burrow entrance. It eats sand at one end and passes it out the other, digesting all the tiny plants and animals in the sand as it passes it through. At the exit of the burrow it intermittently deposits its waste. This leaves a cast on the surface, piled high in spirals, and is a sign of fresh worm activity; casts are made about once every forty minutes. Worms that have casts the colour of the surrounding sand are the easiest to dig up as they indicate a worm that is feeding at the surface, but worms that leave casts made of black or darker sand and piled high are normally difficult to dig up. This is because the large cast indicates a lot of excavation work being done by the worm. This black sand comes from the anoxic layer of sediment, found below the surface sand where there is no oxygen; this layer is normally deep down, sometimes a metre or more.

Collection

There are two methods of collecting lugworms – digging and pumping. The pump works well in wet muddy sand and is quick and effortless compared to digging. However, pumping is practically useless in dry hard sand, and if not used correctly the pump will break and kill more worms than it will take alive. For blow lugworm, the simplest method is to dig a long trench along any given line with lots of casts. The best implement for digging is a short

TIP
Drop the fork load of sand from a few feet up; this will cause the sand to fracture along the burrows made by the worms, making them easier to find.

handled fork, rather than a spade. Spades are not advisable in trenching for lugworms, as they will cut the worms.

It's better to dig worm with a fellow angler, with one digging and the other looking, or you can both dig at the same time and keep any eye on each other's trenches. The best times for digging are from mid-September through to February, but the peak digging time is between November and February. Wellington boots are essential, especially if you are digging around in mud flats, and be very careful not to get stuck. If possible don't dig alone; if you must, check the tides, bring a mobile phone, check the coverage and tell someone where you are going and when you expect to return.

Storage

Most lugworm will stay alive for a day or two if kept cold in the fridge or in a cool box. After returning from the shore place your lugworms on layers of newspaper and pick out any cut or damaged worms. Put the good ones, about twenty or so at a time, on fresh dry newspaper and wrap them; repeat this until you have all your worms sorted. Keep the broken bits if you are going flat fishing, as dab like dead and stale worms. Place all your worms in an old fridge and check them the next day; if the paper is wet change the worms onto dry paper. Alternatively, some people put them into a bucket with a load of coarse sand and a little bit of sea water, mainly to keep them cool and damp.

TIP To keep your home a happy one, do not store your worms in the house fridge; trust me, this will not be tolerated by other fridge users.

You can also freeze lugworms but I have never had much success with them; fresh lugworm is far superior bait since it is the scent trail that gives the lugworm its vital catching ingredient.

Lugworm are an excellent bait for most sea angling species. All flatfish, including flounder, small turbot, brill, megrim, dab and plaice, love lugworm. Indeed, most fish will happily take this bait, but lugworms lose their appeal very quickly on the bottom as all their juices are quickly flushed out of them by the action of the sea and the sea bed, so for this reason baits need to be changed at least every twenty minutes or after a few tentative bites from ever wary fish.

As fresh bait, blow or common lugworms with soft bodies are slightly inferior to black lugworm, which are slightly tougher. In parts of the United Kingdom, black lugworm are also known as yellowtail lugworm. Whichever type you are using, remove most of the sand filled tail by pinching it off between thumb and forefinger, taking care not to take all of it off otherwise the guts will spill out and the bait will be virtually useless. Lugworms can be easily enhanced on the hook by the addition of a small strip of squid or fish at the tip, while using tipped bait will also help keep your worms safely on the hook as they are cast out or on their descent towards the seabed. Some anglers like dipping their lugworm in fish oil such as pilchard or ultra bite and some even spray their baits with WD40, but this is all down to personal preference.

When fishing over a sandy bottom, plaice, whiting, dab, flounder, grey gurnard and the occasional thornback ray can all be caught on the same trace using lugworms or lugworms tipped with fish, squid or a small fillet of sand eel. The trace I use is a one up and two down rig (a boom below the first hook which carries the weight and the two other hooks on a flowing trace) with a small mackerel-type spinner just above the last hook on the trace. I also at-

It's better to dig worm with a fellow angler, with one digging and the other looking, or you can both dig at the same time and keep any eye on each other's trenches.

tach a few fluorescent beads and a small pear shaped silver spoon above the other two hooks. The hooks that I use on this trace are usually Kamazan B940 size 2/0.

Another trace that I use and which is also a great trace for the beginner is a double spreader with a hook about six inches above it; the double spreader is easy to use as it very rarely tangles. On the double spreader the two droppers off the ends of the spreader bar should be fairly long, about a foot each in length; above the hook, which should be in a size 2 to 2/0, use six or eight fluorescent beads and a small silver spoon.

Over rough and broken ground, wrasse, pouting, haddock, coalfish, cod, small ling, whiting, all the gurnards and the occasional pollack will all readily take a lugworm bait. Lugworm is excellent bait for wrasse fishing, and will account for large bags of ballan wrasse in very short periods of time. Two hooks are more than enough to use when fishing wrasse, although nearly all your fish will be caught on the bottom hook. So for this reason it is worth baiting up your top hook with a piece of mackerel; this way you improve your chances of catching a cuckoo wrasse.

You can catch cuckoo wrasse on marine worms but they seem to prefer a piece of mackerel or sand eel as bait. The trace to use over rough or broken ground is slightly different to what you use while sand fishing. Instead of using two hooks off the boom I only use one – this cuts down the number of times you will get stuck on the bottom – and I put two hooks above the boom with beads and small spoons. The snood running off the boom should be about 12 inches long and tied with at least 20 pound mono to allow for snagging on the bottom and the sharp teeth of some of the bigger predatory fish. On the end of the snood I like to use a small mackerel-type spinner with a Kamazan size 2/0 to a 4/0 hook on it.

Fishing for flatfish over sand is always a very relaxing affair. Once the baits and traces are on the bottom, the rods can be left standing against the side of the boat or in the rod holder with the reel in free spool and the ratchet on; then just watch for the bites at the top of the rod. Once you see a bite on your rod, let out line, wait for around thirty seconds, and then engage the reel, tighten the line and lift the rod to set the hook. It is not unusual to catch two and sometimes three flatfish of the same or different species at a time.

Tactics for fishing over rough or broken ground are a good deal different than for fishing over sand. You need to be more attentive to the bites and strike once a bite is registered on the rod tip; otherwise if you miss the bite you will need to retrieve the trace because all the fish attracting juices will be gone from the lugworm after it's bitten.

If you are using a large bait with several worms or a cocktail of baits for bigger species or specimens, then you can and probably should use bait elastic. Shirring elastic is used a lot for good bait presentation and for holding large baits together; it is crucial when shore fishing where long distance casting is required. A good supply of good quality lugworm is essential if you are going to fish a whole day on the sand, preferably dug that morning so that they're in prime condition and up to the task at hand.

Razor fish,
mussels & shrimp

29

Razor fish

Although not often used, probably due to the difficulty in collecting them, razor fish are excellent bait. One of my best day's haddock fishing was done with razor fish, while cod also love them. Collecting razor fish can only be done at low tide on the very largest spring tides.

The razors can be dug, but a much easier way is to put salt or a rich saline mix down their keyhole-shaped burrows; the salt irritates the razor fish so much that it pushes itself out of the burrow to get away and to purge itself in clean water.

When you grab the shell to pull it all the way out of its burrow, don't pull on it too hard or you will break off the fleshy muscle it uses to move itself up and down the burrow; instead, keep a

Razor fish

steady pull on it and after a few seconds the muscle will retract into the shell. Razor fish are best used live, but if they are frozen in good shape they will also work well. Small pieces of razor fish can also be used to tip off softer baits for flatfish.

Mussels

Mussels are among the easiest baits to collect. They are a good bait to use for flatfish species and for ballan wrasse, or while jigging for pollack or cod.

A mussel sausage can easily be cut to the required length with a scissors or a sharp knife once you are ready to use it.

Mussels are abundant all around our rocky coastline and you should have no problems getting a good supply after a few minutes of gathering. After collecting a good supply, I feed them onto the wire, then wrap the mussels in plenty of bait elastic and make a mussel sausage (see the tip on mussels in the section on haddock). The mussel sausage can easily be cut to the required length with a scissors or a sharp knife on the boat or shore once you are ready to use it.

Do not eat mussels that you pick up along the shoreline unless you know for sure that they are fit for human consumption. Clams and cockles can also be prepared and used in the same way as mussels.

Shrimps

Shrimps are another good bait and are easily scooped up with a kid's fishing net. They make excellent bait for pollack and wrasse, and are best used while they are still alive. When out of the water for a few minutes you will notice some of the shrimps will start to go white in colour; these are starting to die, and when dead will turn bright pink in colour. Shrimps

Shrimps

can easily be kept alive in a container with small holes and hung over the side of the boat. By just hooking them by the tail the movement they give off while trying to escape does not go unnoticed and they will not be long on the bottom before coming under attack.

EXCELLENT BAITS: the periwinkle, the limpet and the clam

There are loads of other baits that can be used, including winkles, limpets, barnacles, clams and hermit crabs. As I have said, almost any type of marine creature can be used to catch other aquatic creatures; in the marine world it is a case of eat or be eaten. Baits are always best used alive or as fresh as possible, but you should always keep a good supply frozen for those days when you go fishing on the spur of the moment and do not have time to collect fresh bait.

Sea angling Rods

here is no one rod that is suitable for all types of sea fishing. Rods vary in length and specific line classes to cope with the different fishing techniques and situations that may be encountered. Gone are the days of the old cane, brush handle type rods equipped with a winch of a reel. Back then anglers needed to be built like Popeye just to hold on to the rod for the day, never mind catching any amount of fish on it. Nowadays rods are much lighter and stronger and are made from materials such as glass fibre, carbon fibre, Kevlar and boron, or a mix of these.

When you buy a fishing rod you generally get what you pay for – the more expensive the rod the better the quality, but always get advice before you purchase. If you are a member of a sea angling club or you know an experienced angler, ask them for guidance; a chat for a few minutes could save you a lot of hard earned cash. Most boat rods are generally 8 feet or less as they need to be manageable in the confined spaces of the boat. Exceptions

A selection of rods and reels

are spinning and uptiding rods, which are between 9 and 12 feet in length. Using an uptiding rod is classed as beach fishing from the boat, only with a smaller rod, about 10 feet or so. Spinning rods are soft and flexible, usually around 9 or 10 feet in length and around 12 pound class. These rods need to be flexible as much of their use involves flicking leadheads, lures and ball shot away from the boat.

Beach casting is another element of sea angling which would require a whole book to itself, due to the casting techniques, different areas being fished

Lever drag reel

and the specialised rods and reels involved. Generally, before buying a beach casting outfit you should get some advice from an experienced beach angler, read through beach fishing magazines or do some research on the internet. Find out what type of rod is most suitable for your needs and within your price range. There is no point in buying a special blank and a highly tuned reel if all you want to do is cast it 100 yards or so; all too often novices get caught out by buying overly expensive gear only to discover that this type of sea fishing is not for them.

For beach fishing all you will need is a 12 or 13 foot medium-fast 6 ounce rod that breaks down into two sections, a small multiplier or fixed spool reel, 15 to 18 pound breaking strain reel line and a 50 pound shock leader; the shock leader should be at least twice the length of the rod and then some. (Always use a shock leader; without one your mainline will break and your lead will be like an uncontrolled missile travelling along the beach, taking out everything in its path.) If you know a beach caster then ask him to demonstrate how to cast properly. Never exceed the maximum weight on the rod,

as it could snap during a cast. After a few trips beach fishing you will know whether or not it is the sport for you. Most rods now conform to the IGFA (International Game Fishing Association) line ratings: 12–20 pound class for light fishing, 25–30 pound class for general bottom fishing, 50 pound class for wrecking and 80 pound class for shark and serious conger fishing.

Multiplier with braid

Rod rings should be good quality and

spaced properly; this will not be a problem if you are buying a good brand name rod, as top brand rods usually offer the best back up in the unlikely event of anything going wrong. Expert skill will not overcome a catastrophe if you hook a prospective record-breaker on cheap, second-rate tackle. But also remember that an expensive first-class rod does not and will not make a high quality angler; this can only be achieved through correct use of the rod, and a willingness to learn over time.

Sea angling Reels

When it comes to sea angling there are only two types of reels, a fixed spool reel and a multiplier reel, but there are literally thousands of each type to choose from. There are several top quality brands but among the best are those manufactured by Penn, whose reels are of excellent quality and built for the tough environment of the sea angler. In the case of the multiplier reel, as its name suggests, the reel's gearing multiplies the spool's revolutions for each turn of the handle; this is used for distance beach casting and boat fishing.

Spinning reel

Multiplier reels are usually classed by their drag systems and line load; the drag system is either star drag or the superior lever drag system, which allows easier control over hard-fighting fish. Fixed spool reels are usually used for spinning from piers, basic beach fishing, rock fishing and spinning from the boat. The fixed spool reel provides problem-free casting, which makes this type of reel the perfect choice for the beginner. Line class usually classes these reels according to what their workload should be; the better quality reels will have brass components and a good number of ball bearings among their many moving parts.

Rod and reel

Line .

There are also a few types of line to choose from. The top ones are monofilament, braid and wire, although wire line is becoming dated and will probably
soon disappear from the market. There are many different types of braid on
the market; most are superb but beware of no brand line. Braid is excellent
in that there is absolutely no stretch with it, it is ultra thin, and you can feel
every bite, knock and touch like no other line before it. The only problem
is that if you get tangled with a fellow angler or get stuck on the bottom, a
tangle with braid usually results in someone having to cut their line because
it is so difficult to unravel it.

If you are unfortunate enough to get stuck on the bottom using braid,
under no circumstances should you wrap it around your hand or fingers as
braid has the potential to sever fingers from the hand. I always carry a piece
of stick in my tackle box; actually it's the shaft of a hammer, with which I
administer the last rites to any fish that is destined for the table. This piece

of wood can be used to take a few turns of braid to pull your trapped gear off the bottom. Monofilament, on the other hand, has an abundance of elasticity, which makes it excellent for spinning and for tying traces; it gives most big fish enough leeway not to snap your trace. Monofilament is also the only line that works properly on fixed spool reels, and all novices should use monofilament on their reels until they get enough confidence and experience to try the no-nonsense braid.

Sea angling traces

There are about half a dozen traces that will cover all your boat-angling needs. Now that you have read about each species you can refer to which traces work best for each one. Try not to over elaborate on your traces, as they will usually end up tangled or, worse still, spook all but the dumbest of fish. Hook size and sharpness is the most important thing,

Star drag reel

but it's also crucial to have them tied correctly with proper knots and, of course, with good quality line. Do not attempt to tie your traces with line if it has just been bought from the shop window; direct sunlight ruins monofilament so make sure it comes out of a box and not from the display. Always try to buy decent quality line for tying your traces.

Top Locations

All around the British Isles we are gifted with a larger segment of the continental shelf compared to the rest of our European neighbours, giving us a larger area for fishing and the possibility of catching more species. Not all fish are resident in our seas throughout the year; many follow the Gulf Stream, a current of water with a higher temperature that comes

Bluefin tuna

closer to our shores during the summer months. Numerous species travel with this warmer current to reproduce or while following their food, and they in turn are followed by other larger predatory species such as dolphins, bluefin tuna, bonito, sharks and whales. To see dolphins leaping out of the water and riding the crest of the bow waves created by a boat is something that will stay with you forever.

There are some excellent locations for fishing different species and incredible scenery around the Irish coast. Some species grow to bigger sizes, require different tactics or fight better in different locations. Haddock, for instance, grow bigger and fight much harder around Tory island than in any other area; the bluefin tuna fishing from Killybegs and Downings is indescribable, with more tuna caught here than in some of the big angling venues in the southern hemisphere, while the elusive tope is prolific around Lough Swilly and Downings. Some of the best vessels and locations to fish in Ireland are listed here.

Wreck Hunter II

Sea angling around the Old Head of Kinsale and Ballycotton Bay is excellent all year round; mackerel, pollock, conger, ling, coalfish, cod, whiting, haddock, pouting, wrasse, blue shark, blonde and thornback ray, gurnard, plaice and dab are all on the menu. One particular boat I like to fish on is the *Wreck Hunter II*, a new custom built Wildcat 107 catamaran, skippered by Joe Lynch who has been involved in charter sea angling for many years. He operates all year round (weather permitting!) from Salve Marine Marina, in the centre of Crosshaven, which is just inside the entrance to Cork harbour, and fishes on the wrecks and reefs from west of the Old Head of Kinsale to east of Ballycotton bay and up to forty miles offshore.

> CONTACT: Joe Lynch on Tel: 00 353 87 230 2362;
> E-mail: joelynch@iol.ie

Rooster

Baltimore in west Cork is a centre for reef, wreck and shark fishing. Reef marks include the Stags, Fastnet Rock and Mizen Head. The Stags, in particular, is a noted skate mark with some fish here exceeding 200 pounds. The *Rooster* is a fast, modern offshore 105 charter boat, built to the skipper's specifications, and meets the latest safety standards; the boat and skipper are fully licensed and committed to the job. Some of the wrecks fished include the largest wreck in European waters, the 160,000 ton *Kowloon Bridge*, and numerous wartime wrecks which are havens for specimen ling, conger, cod, pollack and coalfish. From June to September there is a good run of blue shark, with porbeagle and six-gilled shark putting in the occasional appearance; a rod-caught six-gilled shark of 315 pounds was caught here (more than double the record for the species). In late summer, albacore tuna also come within range; a catch of twenty-one albacore was taken by anglers off Baltimore in 2004.

> CONTACT: Nick Dent on Tel: 00 353 86 824 0642
> E-mail: nick@wreckfish.com

Tigger

The Beara peninsula is a 45-kilometre-long peninsula jutting out from the south west of Ireland into the clear blue waters of the Atlantic ocean. John and Maree Angles run Inches House angling centre based on the peninsula. They have three Fáilte Ireland-approved self catering holiday cottages and a 31-foot fast pro charter offshore angling vessel called *Tigger*. It is fully licensed to operate up to thirty miles from the port of Castletownbere where it is based. Species include pollack, coalfish, cod, mackerel, conger eel, haddock, whiting, ling, ballan and cuckoo wrasse, thornback ray, blonde ray, spotted ray, turbot, brill, plaice, dab, megrim, gurnard, bass, blue shark and many others. Over two hundred rays were tagged and released in the last three seasons here (from 2003 to 2006).

CONTACT: John on Tel/Fax: 00 353 27 74494, Mob: 00 353 86 398 3856
Email: info@irelandseaangling.com

Lagosta II

Based at Loughcarrig House, the East Cork Angling Centre offers a fast turbo offshore 105 35-foot purpose built angling boat, *Lagosta II*. This is a perfect base for an Irish angling holiday, with all the home comforts including drying room, freezer facilities and tackle storage. Loughcarrig House is situated on the shores of Cork harbour and is located just three miles from Midleton in Co. Cork. The centre is ideal for a day's or week's sea fishing to chase that specimen catch at wreck, or for reef and shark fishing, and they have almost a hundred specimen catches to their credit. Specimen cod, pollack, ray, conger, flats and many other species are always on the cards here. The house is also the base for the East Cork Bird Watch Centre.

CONTACT: Brian or Cheryl Byrne on Tel: 00 353 21 463 1952
E-mail: info@loughcarrig.com

Harpy, Kinsale, Co. Cork

Cork Harbour Boats

Cork Harbour Boats operate from the historic town of Cobh, which commands panoramic views of Cork harbour – one of the finest natural and well sheltered harbours in the world. The *Cuan Ban*, an aqua-star, and the *Castle Maiden*, an offshore 105 angling boat, are both skippered by experienced fishermen. There have been a number of impressive catches here, including blue shark, pollack, ling, cod, conger eel, coalfish, wrasse, whiting, mackerel, ray, plaice, dab, turbot and many others.

Full tackle hire is also available.

CONTACT: Tel: 00 353 21 484 1348 or 00 353 21 484 1633;
Fax: 00 353 21 484 1348; Mobile: 00 353 87 236 3566
E-mail: corkharbourboatsltd@eircom.net

Harpy and Sundance Kid

There are two licensed charter boats based at Kinsale, Co. Cork – a 43-foot aqua-star called *Harpy*, owned and skippered by Willem Jan van Dijk, and a 38 foot aqua-star, *Sundance Kid*, owned and skippered by Butch Roberts. Both vessels operate all year round, and a lot of reef, bottom and wreck fishing down to 120 metres is done here throughout the year. Sharks are also targeted during the summer months. Common species caught include pollack, coalfish, cod, ling, whiting, gurnard, conger, dogfish, bull huss, ballan and cuckoo wrasse, mackerel, herring, ray and blue shark.

> **CONTACT:** Willem on Tel: 00 353 21 477 8944;
> Mobile: 00 353 87 988 2839.

Sioux

Valentia Fishing has been operating a deep sea angling business for the last ten years. Siegy Grabher and his angling boat *Sioux* an offshore 105, which is licensed to carry twelve passengers, takes great satisfaction in getting anglers the very best fishing on their day out, and excellent sport is a guarantee. Most of the fishing is carried out around Valentia island, Skellig islands, the Blasket islands and Dingle bay which has spectacular scenery as well as excellent fishing. Catches are mainly pollack, mackerel, cod, coalfish, haddock, whiting, ling, conger, blue shark, skate, ray, dogfish, bull huss, pouting, wrasse, gurnard, garfish and bass. Over the last few years the *Sioux* has caught the first blue sharks of the season around Valentia island. A tag and release policy is adopted here on all the blue sharks and skates, and all the information on the sharks and skates is sent to the Central Fisheries Board.

> **CONTACT:** Siegy on Tel/Fax: 00 353 66 947 6420
> Mobile: 00 353 87 687 1267; E-mail: siegygrabher@eircom.net

Clare Dragoon

The *Clare Dragoon* is a purpose built 37-foot Lochin 366 and is owned and run by Luke Aston at the Carrigaholt Sea Angling Centre. The angling centre is based in the fishing village of Carrigaholt on the south side of loop head peninsula, where the Shannon estuary meets the affluent fishing grounds of Ireland's south west coast and, as it is in an estuary, it is possible to go fishing in all weather conditions. Carrigaholt Sea Angling Centre is owned and run by Mary and Luke Aston. Mary could also take care of your accommodation needs in 'Glencarrig' guest house. The sea angling centre offers great fishing packages for up to eight fishermen at a time. Carrigaholt is about one and a half hours' drive from Shannon airport and you can arrange with Luke or Mary to get collected there. Luke also writes regular fishing reports for the Shannon Regional Fisheries Board.

CONTACT: Luke or Mary on Tel: 00 353 65 905 8209
Mobile: 00 353 87 636 7544; E-mail: lukeaston@eircom.net

Deora Dé

Deora Dé is a fast modern 35-foot offshore 105 charter boat based at Schull and is skippered by Jim Linehan. *Deora Dé* is built to the skipper's own specifications and meets all current safety standards. Species of fish caught include blue shark, mackerel, pollack, cod, whiting, conger eel, ling, wrasse, gurnard, garfish, dogfish and coalfish. Rod and tackle hire is available with free tuition given. Free tea and coffee onboard. The *Deora Dé* is capable of operating thirty nautical miles of Ballycotton – Cork Harbour – Kinsale.

CONTACT: Jim on 00 353 21 486 3445; Mobile: 00 353 86 409 1389
E-mail: mohawkangling@eircom.net; Website: www.deora-de.pro.ie

Valentia Fishing, Co. Kerry

Sharpshooter

The *Sharpshooter* is a 38-foot Aquastar which is skippered by John O'Connor and is based at Dunmore East in Co. Waterford. This part of the Irish coast has a large number of wrecks which are within an hour of Dunmore East. The skipper has many years of experience and has accumulated a wealth of knowledge in all types of fishing. Wreck, reef and shark fishing are the norm here and evening trips and rod hire can be easily organised with the skipper. Tuition is free. Bass, coalfish, cod, conger, dab, flounder, garfish, gurnards, haddock, ling, pollack, pouting, scad, blue shark, ballan wrasse, cuckoo wrasse are caught on a regular basis.

CONTACT: Tel: 00 353 51 383397; Mobile: 00 353 87 268 2794; Fax 00 353 51 383397.

Hanna K

The *Hanna K* is an Offshore 105 and is skippered by Michael Fahey and Pat Wade who between them have a wealth of knowledge on fishing in the area. This vessel is based in Dungarvan, Co. Waterford and specialises in wreck, reef and shark fishing. You can expect to catch bass, coalfish, cod, conger, dab, flounder, garfish, gurnards, haddock, ling, pollack, pouting, scad, blue shark, ballan wrasse, cuckoo wrasse, turbot, brill and plaice.

CONTACT: Tel: 00 353 58 46577;
Mobile: 00 353 87 6897600 or 00 353 86 819 1074

Deep Sea Charters

Deep Sea Charters is the home of the *Keltoi Warrior*, an Interceptor 38 which is a high-tech charter boat available for hire in the picturesque south-eastern waters of Ireland. It is based in Dunmore East, Co. Waterford. Blue sharks are caught here from mid June to October, with the peak period being between July and September. Cod, pollack, wrasse, bull huss, bass, conger, tope, ray, ling, dab, plaice and flounder are all prolific here.

CONTACT: Brendan on 00 353 87 636 9164; Mobile: 00 353 87 260 8917
E-mail: info@deepseachartersdunmore.com

Avoca

The *Avoca*, a 33-foot Lochin, is skippered by John Tynan and is based at Dungarvan in Co. Waterford. Dungarvan was once a major angling destination in the late 70s and early 80s and is now undergoing something of a revival in the sport because of the good fishing grounds and new investment in charter boats. Dungarvan is also one of Ireland's top spots for blue shark angling; sharks are plentiful here from mid-June until mid-October. Other species you are likely to catch are whiting, haddock, coalfish, bull huss, dogfish, rays, plaice, brill, and wrasse, ling, conger, pollack and cod.

CONTACT: 00 353 58 42657; Mobile: 00 353 86 839 2624; Fax: 00 353 58 42657

Osprey

The *Osprey* is a 43-foot Aquastar and is powered by a Catapillar 350 HP engine. The vessel is skippered by Maurice McGrath and is based at Dungarvan in Co. Waterford. The *Osprey* specialises in reef, wreck, shark and general inshore angling catching species like pollack, mackerel, cod, coalfish, haddock, whiting, ling, conger, blue shark, skates, rays, dogfish, bullhuss, pouting, wrasse, gurnard, garfish and bass.

CONTACT: 00 353 58 44129; Mobile: 00 353 86 817 7829

Autumn Dream

The *Autumn Dream* is a 38-foot Offshore 115 which is owned and skippered by Eamonn Hayes and is based at Kilmore Quay in Co. Wexford. Kilmore Quay is a small fishing village situated on the south east corner of Ireland and is only fifteen kilometres from Rosslare ferry port. The *Autumn Dream* specialises in reef, wreck, ray, tope and general inshore angling, the current Irish record for red mullet was caught on this boat.

CONTACT: 00 353 53 9129723; Mobile: 00 353 87 213530
Fax: 00 353 53 9129614

Lady Alison

The *Lady Alison* is a 33-foot Aquastar based at Kilmore Quay in Co. Wexford and is skippered by Paul Bates. Bass, codling, coalfish, dogfish, ray, flounder garfish, gurnards, haddock, ling, pollack, pouting, scad, blue shark, ballan wrasse and cuckoo wrasse are caught on a regular basis on this boat.

CONTACT: 00 353 53 9129831; Mobile: 00 353 86 2075901
Fax: 00 353 53 9145888.

Fiona Tee

Skippered by PJ Bates the *Fiona Tee*, a 33-foot Fast Fisherman, is a new state of the art angling boat designed to the skipper's exact requirements. The *Fiona Tee* is based in the small fishing village of Kilmore Quay in Co. Wexford and can operate up to twenty miles out from the harbour over the best wrecks and reefs.

CONTACT: 00 353 53 9129896; Mobile: 00 353 86 3839500
Fax: 00 353 53 91429704.

Sailfish

The *Sailfish* is a Mitchell 31 and is owned and skippered by Leslie Bates. The *Sailfish* is based at Kilmore Quay in Co. Wexford. Fishing over reef, wrecks and clean ground is the norm here as well as a good deal of tope and ray fishing. Evening trips are also available. Species caught regularly here include pollack, mackerel, cod, coalfish, haddock, whiting, ling, conger, blue shark, skates, rays, dogfish, bullhuss, pouting, wrasse, gurnard, garfish and bass.

CONTACT: 00 353 53 9129806; Mobile: 00 353 87 2492718
Fax: 00 353 53 9129806

Red Dragon

The *Red Dragon* is skippered by Adrian and Noel Furlong and is based at Kilmore Quay in Co. Wexford. The *Red Dragon* operates to thirty miles out of Kilmore Quay and specimen sized pollack, cod, coalfish, haddock, whiting, ling, conger, ray, dogfish, bull huss, pouting, ballan wrasse, cuckoo wrasse, gurnard, megrim, turbot, brill, plaice and dab are all caught here.

CONTACT: 00 353 51 563242; Mobile: 00 353 87 6545529.

Wild Swan

The *Wild Swan* is a 42-foot Interceptor vessel Owned and operated by Jim Foley a professional skipper with many years experience of the local fishing area, it is based at Duncannon in Co. Wexford. Wreck fishing and general ground angling will produce excellent mixed catches of conger, ling, pollack, coalfish and cod. Shark fishing will provide good sport with catches of up to 100 pounds during summer months.

CONTACT: 00 353 51 389225; Mobile: 00 353 87 6781245
Fax: 00 353 51 389225.

Kilquade

The *Kilquade* is a 24m ex-Clovelly Class Fleet Tender and is skippered by Gordon Hunter. The vessel is based at Wicklow Harbour and operates off the Wicklow and Dublin coasts. This large charter vessel offers ample deck space for twelve anglers with excellent on-board facilities. Species caught regularly here include pollack, mackerel, cod, coalfish, haddock, whiting, ling, conger, blue shark, skates, rays, dogfish, bullhuss, pouting, wrasse, gurnard, garfish and bass.

CONTACT: 00 353 1 2877260; Mobile: 00 353 87 2590175.

Prospector 1

The *Prospector 1* is a purpose built state of the art 33-foot Lochin charter angling vessel and is owned and skippered by Peter Power who has been a keen angler for over thirty years. The *Prospector 1* fishes in Donegal Bay from the idyllic harbour of Mullaghmore, County Sligo, in the summer months (May through October) and in Dublin Bay, from Howth harbour, County Dublin, in the winter months (November through April).

CONTACT: 00 353 1 8430380; Mobile: 00 353 87 2576268
Fax: 00 353 1 8430381

Brazen Hussy, West coast

Adam Patricia

The *Adam Patricia* is a 35-foot Freeward and is owned and skippered by Frank and Ken Doyle. This vessel is based at Howth in County Dublin and operates up to fifteen miles north or south of Howth and up to three miles from land. Bass, codling, coalfish, dogfish, ray, flounder, garfish, gurnards, haddock, ling, pollack, pouting, scad, blue shark, ballan wrasse, cuckoo wrasse and mackerel are caught here on a regular basis.

CONTACT: 00 353 87 2678211; Mobile: 00 353 87 6573832.

Lady Clare

The *Lady Clare* is a Lochin 33 and is skippered by Darragh Scott. The vessel is based at Malahide Marina in Co. Dublin and can operate up to thirty miles off the coast at Malahide or Dun Laoghaire. Species caught here include pollack, mackerel, cod, coalfish, haddock, whiting, ling, conger, blue shark, skates, rays, dogfish, bullhuss, pouting, wrasse, gurnard, garfish and bass.

CONTACT: Mobile: 00 353 87 2334244; 00 353 86 306 1236
Fax: 00 353 1 8462085

James Owen

The *James Owen* is a Mitchell 31 and is skippered by Pat Rankin, a professional skipper with many years experience of the local fishing areas. The vessel is based at Dundalk in Co. Louth, can operate up to thirty miles out to sea and specialises in reef inshore and tope fishing.

CONTACT: 00 353 42 933 9695; Mobile: 00 353 87 942 7146

Brazen Hussy

For any enthusiastic angler, fishing off the west coast of Ireland presents a wide variety of opportunities. On an average day out with Shane Bisgood on the *Brazen Hussy*, you can expect to catch between eight and ten different species of fish, with the very real possibility that the next fish will be a specimen. Equipment is available for hire should you be travelling light and there are a number of facilities on board to make it a very pleasant day at sea. The *Brazen Hussy* is rigged as a scuba dive boat, angling boat and general touring vessel, taking people out to the numerous islands off the Connemara coast; these include High island, Inishbofin, Inishshark, Inishturk and Clare island. The *Brazen Hussy* normally operates from Derryinver or Cleggan harbours and the vessel may be chartered by the hour or for a discounted rate by the day.

CONTACT: Shane on Tel: 00 353 86 279 5118; E-mail: brazencharter@gmail.com

Bru Chlann Lir

'Bru Chlann Lir' is a modern dormer bungalow situated on the beautiful un-spoilt Mullet peninsula and has two sea angling vessels, the *Noirín Bán*, a 38-foot bullet skippered by John O'Boyle and the *Fionnula*, a 33-foot Lochin skippered by Mattie Geraghty. 'Brú Chlann Lir' offers the perfect getaway for anglers, with two charter boats and experienced skippers who will take you to some of the best sea angling areas in Europe. The local area boasts over forty species of fish and a huge choice of waters, from sheltered inlets to Achill head where the reefs are home to some large predatory fish. Sand banks with plenty of pan sized plaice and big hard hitting pollack are numerous, while ballan wrasse are an everyday occurrence at the Black Rock – a must for any angler.

CONTACT: Tel: 00 353 97 85741
E-mail: bruclannlir@eircom.net

The Lady Marlyn

A Lochin 40 owned and skippered by Pat Conneely, the *Lady Marlyn* can accommodate twelve anglers in comfort. The boat is based at Roundstone harbour, Co. Galway and is just a short trip away from the prolific fishing reefs there. The Atlantic waters off Roundstone yield huge numbers of many species, including pollack, ling, cod, coalfish, wrasse, mackerel, ray, plaice, dab and turbot. A day's fishing can often yield over twenty different species and many groups thoroughly enjoy a 'species hunt' competition. Shark fishing is also very popular; blue sharks up to 150 pounds have been caught regularly and porbeagle can also be found in these waters. Pat's wife, Margaret, runs the 'Harbour View' B&B in Roundstone, which offers superb accommoda-tion and is Bord Failte approved. Many groups choose to stay with the skip-per where they can discuss the day's fishing and plan their next trip. The boat is also equipped with a 'fighting chair' for the giant blue fin tuna that can sometimes be found off-shore.

CONTACT: Pat Conneely on Tel: 00 353 95 35952
Mobile: 00 353 87 287 1012; E-mail: roundstoneangling@hotmail.com

Nuala Star, Killybegs, Co. Donegal

Doloree

The *Doloree* is a fast offshore 105, 35-foot boat which is owned and skippered by Sean Lavelle and based at Belmullet in Co. Mayo. Belmullet is one of the best all-round sea angling centres in Ireland with over forty varieties of fish known to inhabit the surrounding waters. The sea angler is well rewarded here with some of the best all-round angling in the sheltered waters of Blacksod bay to the south and Broad Haven bay to the north. The Achill island area offers excellent deep sea fishing with the Irish records for both porbeagle shark (365 pounds) and blue shark (256 pounds) held there. Belmullet also holds the Irish record for tub gurnard (12lb 3ozs), red gurnard (3lb 9ozs) and halibut (156 pounds). Belmullet holds a two-day competition at the end of August each year; this competition is fantastic and is a must for any angler wanting to catch plenty of species.

CONTACT: Sean Lavelle on Mobile: 00 353 86 836 5983
E-mail: seanlavelle@eircom.net

Naomh Carta

Naomh Carta is an 38-foot Interceptor owned and skippered by Adrian Molloy who is based at Kilcar and operates in Donegal bay and up to thirty miles out. Adrian has over twenty years' experience in both commercial fishing and sea angling off the north west coast of Ireland and is renowned for his uncanny ability to track and catch the mighty bluefin tuna. He has caught several huge specimens and is currently the Irish record holder with a bluefin tuna catch weighing 440 kilogrammes.

CONTACT: Adrian Tel: 00 353 74 973 8377; Mobile: 00 353 87 227 6396; Fax: 00 353 74 973 8535; E-mail: adrian@tunacharters.ie; Web: www.tunacharters.ie

Bluefin Charters

The angling boat, *Kiwi Girl*, is a fast Kingfisher Sport Hunter owned and skippered by Liam Carey and is located at Mullaghmore, Co. Sligo on the northwest coast of Ireland. Whether you are an experienced angler or a mere beginner, Liam makes it a point to see that you enjoy your time onboard with him. He successfully tutors junior and novice anglers on how best to catch their quarry – so much so, in fact, that a thirteen-year-old boy called Michael Conway caught a blue shark weighing over 130 pounds.

The *Kiwi Girl* fishes all around Donegal bay and has had some fantastic catches, including a common skate weighing in at 151 pounds as well as some specimen size pollack, cod, coalfish, haddock, whiting, ling, conger, ray, dogfish, bull huss, pouting, wrasse, gurnard, megrim, turbot, brill, plaice and dab. Big game fishing for shark and giant bluefin has taken off in Donegal bay in recent years and *Kiwi Girl* is built for the challenge. If you intend to go sea angling on the north west coast of Ireland, book yourself on the *Kiwi Girl* – you will not regret it.

CONTACT: Liam on Tel: 00 353 71 916 6106. Boat/ Mobile: 00 353 87 257 4497; E-mail: liammcarey@eircom.net

Fisherman's Village Lodge

Rosguill is a state of the art 43-foot Aqua-star based at Downings, north Donegal and is owned and skippered by Michael McVeigh. Within forty miles of Downings there are 109 wrecks that can be fished, including the *Audacious*, a dreadnought battleship of 23,000 tons, and the *Justicia* of 32,000 tons. There is also some spectacular fishing around Tory island which is renowned for the quality of its reef fishing and a great place to go in strong winds for sheltered fishing. Some of the best bottom fishing in Ireland is done here over reefs, clean and mixed ground. The *Rosguill* catches over forty species each year, including blue shark and my favourite, the halibut. Michael has also caught several bluefin tuna, one weighing a massive 507 pounds. Heather runs the 'Fisherman's Village Lodge', which is set on the spectacular Atlantic drive, three miles north of Downings. This is one of my all time favourite fishing locations because of the sheer volume of fish and species that I hook into.

CONTACT: Michael or Heather on Tel: 00 353 74 915 5080;
E-mail: info@rosguill.com

Pinalia

The *Pinalia* is a 31-foot Versatility owned and skippered by Pat O'Callaghan. Based in Killybegs, the *Pinalia* fishes all around Donegal bay. A general day's fishing with Pat will see you catch pollack, cod, ling, coalies, pouting, John Dory, turbot, brill, blonde, thornback, homelyn, cuckoo ray, plaice, megrims, dab, gurnard, spurdog, ballan and cuckoo wrasse, dogfish, bull huss, tope, conger eel, angler fish, blue shark and the occasional bass.

CONTACT: Pat on Tel: 00 353 74 973 1569; Mobile: 00 353 86 860 0736;
Fax: 00 353 74 973 1691; E-mail: pocfish@email.com

Nuala Star

The *Nuala Star* is a 36-foot fiberglass Ocean tramp and is based at Teelin pier on the north side of Donegal bay twelve miles from Killybegs. The skipper, Paddy Byrne, has over twenty years' experience in both commercial fishing and leisure angling and has caught some specimen size pollack, cod, coalfish, haddock, whiting, ling, conger, ray, dogfish, bull huss, pouting, wrasse, gurnard, megrim, turbot, brill, plaice and dab. The scenery here is stunning, with impressive views of Sliabh Liag and Bunglas, Europe's highest sea cliffs. Paddy also picks you up in designated areas for a small extra fee. Places like Killybegs, Bundoran or indeed Mullaghmore are no problem, or indeed most harbours on Donegal bay.

CONTACT: Tel: 00 353 74 973 9365; Mobile: 00 353 87 6284668;
E-mail: nualastarteelin@hotmail.com or paddy.byrne@nualastarteelin.com

Duanai Mara

The *Duanai Mara* is a 33-foot Delta star Pro Angler owned by the Creevy and District community cooperative society and skippered by Smith Campbell. The sea angling in this area is quite varied with a huge number of species available, from pollack, cod, ling, coalie, pouting, John Dory, turbot, ray, plaice, dab, gurnard, spurdog, ballan and cuckoo wrasse, dogfish, bull huss, tope, conger eel and angler fish and occasionally bass, triggerfish, blue shark and, of course, the blue fin tuna. The *Duanai Mara* is moored in Killybegs, but can pick up anglers from Killybegs harbour, Creevy pier, Mullaghmore and Teelin pier. Smith Campbell is also secretary of the Northwest Charter Skippers Association, which is a group of twelve charter boat operators working in the Donegal bay and surrounding areas.

CONTACT: Tel/Fax: 00 353 71 985 2896; 00 353 74 973 9889;
Mobile: 00 353 87 275 9731; E-mail: smithcampbell@eircom.net;
Website: www.duanaimaracharters.com

An Shannen Alainn

An Shannen Alainn is a Rodman 1250 owned and skippered by Michael Molloy and operates in Donegal bay. Michael can take you sea angling for blue shark, bluefin tuna, wreck fishing and general sea angling, catching you many species such as pollack, ling, cod, coalfish, wrasse, mackerel, ray, plaice, dab, turbot and many others. A day's fishing can often yield over twenty different species and many groups thoroughly enjoy species hunting with him. Sightseeing trips are also available here.

CONTACT: Michael on 00 353 74 973 8495; Mobile: 00 353 87 206 6513; E-mail: smmolloy@yahoo.com; Website: www.bluefin.ie

Killybegs Angling Charters

Killybegs Angling Charters is based at the Blackrock pier in Killybegs, Co. Donegal. The *MV Meridian* is a 40-foot Lochin purpose built for sea angling and is owned and skippered by Brian McGilloway. Brian has over thirty years' experience in charter angling and is chairman of the Killybegs sea angling club. The *MV Meridian* can take you fishing for cod, pollack, ling, conger, brill, turbot, plaice, all the ray species, bull huss, tope, conger, ballan and cuckoo wrasse, dogfish, blue sharks and now even bluefin tuna – the first bluefin tuna ever taken on rod and line in Irish waters was caught aboard the *MV Suzanne* (Brian's former boat) by Alan Glanville. The boat leaves daily for full or half-day angling charters and sightseeing trips of the bay or longer trips to the cliffs of Sliabh Liag.

CONTACT: Tel: 00 353 74 973 1144; Mobile: 00 353 87 220 0982; E-mail: killybegsanglingcharters@oceanfree.net; Website: www.killybegsangling. com

Deep Sea Charters, Dunmore East, Co. Waterford

Huntress Blue

The *Huntress Blue*, a steel hull 30-foot vessel owned and skippered by Michael McGettigan, is based at Killybegs and operates in Donegal bay. Michael can take you to any type of fishing that you like, including species such as coalfish, cod, ling, ballan wrasse, cuckoo wrasse, conger, pouting, whiting, scad, garfish, John Dory, bull huss, dogfish, tope, blue shark, flounder, dab, plaice, megrim, turbot and brill, with occasional haddock and spurdog. If you are after specimen ling, conger or pollack then look no further. Michael has an uncanny talent for catching specimen sized fish; he will tell you what works well and teaches juniors and novices in the art of sea angling. He can also make a mean cup of coffee.

CONTACT: Telephone: 00 353 74 973 1401; Mobile: 00 353 87 287 1423;
E-mail: huntressblue@eircom.net

Summer Rose

The *Summer Rose* is skippered and owned by Sammie Scott and is based in Downings, Co. Donegal. The skipper has over twenty-five years' experience and has accumulated a wealth of knowledge in all types of fishing. There are a large number of ship wrecks off the Donegal coast. Between Arranmore Island and west of Portrush there lies a total of 138 recorded wrecks and Sammie knows which ones fish best. Sammie was recently presented with a plaque from *Sea Angler* magazine in recognition of running a first-class charter boat that gives both service and value for money.

CONTACT: Tel: 00 353 74 915 5386; E-mail: sammyscott@eircom.net

Enterprise I and Swilly Explorer

The *Enterprise I* is a 38-foot Aqua star and the *Swilly Explorer* is a 42-foot Interceptor; both are based in Rathmullan in Co. Donegal. These two vessels are skippered by Neil Doherty and Angela Crerand, two accomplished skippers and sea anglers in their own right. Reef, wreck, tope and general inshore fishing is all done here. The tope fishing here is second to none, with good numbers tagged and released every year. Wreck fishing is normally done on the 570-foot,15,000 ton liner, the *Laurentic*, which sank on 25 January 1917 after it struck a German-laid mine at the entrance to Lough Swilly; it was carrying a staggering £5 million sterling in gold bars at the time. Pollack, cod, ling, coalie, pouting, John Dory, turbot, ray, plaice, dab, gurnard, spurdog, ballan and cuckoo wrasse, dogfish, bull huss, tope, conger eel, angler fish, triggerfish, blue shark and blue fin tuna are all caught here.

CONTACT: 00 353 74 58129; Mobile: 00 353 87 263 4107;
E-mail: rathmullencharters@eircom.net

Bonito

The *Bonito* is a 33-foot Cygnus Cyfish owned and skippered by Trevor Ryder and is based at Downings in Co. Donegal. Fishing out of Downings means an angler has the choice of shallow reefs or deep water bottom fishing for numerous species, sandy bottoms for 'flatties', and plenty of wrecks for pollock, ling and conger. Some of these wrecks are rarely fished and hold an abundance of big fish. There are deep water reefs for conger eels, and also cod, whiting, haddock, coalfish, poor cod, grey gurnard, red gurnard, tub gurnard, plaice, turbot, brill, dab, flounder, megrim, thornback ray, undulate ray, blonde ray, cuckoo ray, ballan wrasse, cuckoo wrasse, lesser spotted dogfish, tope, blue shark, blue fin tuna, garfish, pouting, common skate, Amoco Jack and John Dory.

CONTACT: Tel: 00 353 74 9155261; Mobile: 00 353 87 6547232;
E-mail: tryder@eircom.net; Web: www.bonitocharters.com

Barracuda

The *Barracuda* is a 33-foot Lochin which is skippered by John McLoughlin and based at Culdaff in Co. Donegal. There are numerous wrecks which fish well here and most lay within an easy thirty-minutes to one-hour steam. There are no long boring journeys prior to fishing here. You just have time to tackle up and ready yourself and it is time to fish. There has been minimal commercial fishing here due to the fast tides and deep water. Specimen size pollack, cod, coalfish, haddock, whiting, ling, conger, ray, dogfish, bull huss, pouting, wrasse, gurnard, megrim, turbot, brill, plaice and dab are all caught here.

CONTACT: John at: 00 353 74 937 0605; Mobile: 00 353 86 252 2685
E-mail: malininfo@inishowenmotors.ie

Surose, Burtonport, Co. Donegal

Surose

The *Surose*, a Mitchell 31, is skippered by Oscar Duffy and is based at Burton-port, Co. Donegal. Oscar has been operating the *Surose* for several years and is licensed to carry ten passengers. Most of his fishing is done inshore on the many reefs around Arranmore and Owey islands. The sand fishing is out-standing and species hunting a regular event. The shark fishing here in mid-summer is excellent and species regularly caught include pollack, coalfish, cod, ling, ballan wrasse, cuckoo wrasse, conger, pouting, whiting, scad, garfish, John Dory, megrim, haddock, blue shark, flounder, dab, plaice, turbot, brill and dogfish, with the occasional tope and spurdog.

CONTACT: Telephone: 00 353 74 955 1533; 00 353 74 954 2245; or 00 353 87 925 3534; E-mail: liam@inish.ie; Website: www.inish.ie

Loinnir

The *Loinnir* is a 43-foot Aquastar owned and skippered by Neil Gallagher and is based in Burtonport and Bunbeg. Neil has had several specimen catches while charter fishing, including pollack, cuckoo wrasse and blue shark, and a specimen torsk of 8.5 pounds was caught on a wreck by Derek Harris from the Stella Maris Sea angling club. Several other torsk were caught just under the specimen weight.

Over forty species are recorded on this vessel each year; I've caught more species here in one day than anywhere else that I've ever fished. The sand fishing is also excellent here with large turbot, brill and plaice regular features in the catch. Neil regularly takes anglers wreck fishing as there are many shipwrecks located off this part of the Irish coast from the Spanish Armada and from two world wars.

CONTACT: 00 353 74 954 8403; Mobile: 00 353 86 833 2969;
E-mail: info@donegalseaangling.com; Website: www.donegalseaangling.com

The Brothers

The Brothers is owned and skippered by Quinton Nelson and is based at Donaghadee three miles south of Bangor, Co. Down. Quinton has been operating passenger boats out of Donaghadee for thirty-five years and was a regular crewmember on the Donaghadee lifeboat for eighteen years. Fish regularly caught by this boat are cod, whiting, mackerel, pollack, coalfish, gurnard, plaice, dab, dogfish, wrasse, and flounder. Make sure your gear is in good order as a commercial trawler caught a conger eel in excess of 250 pounds weight at Rathlin Island on the coast here several years ago.

CONTACT: 0289 1883 4030; Mobile: 00 44 7811 230215.

Sharon Michélé

The *Sharon Michélé* is an Aqua Star 33 and is skippered by Oliver Finnegan. Oliver is an experienced seaman and a keen angler with an eye for new marks, techniques and species and has succeeded in landing a large number of Irish specimen fish. The *Sharon Michélé* is based at Carlingford lough and can operate up to thirty miles out.

CONTACT: 00 353 28 30264906; Mobile: 00 44 7703 606498.

The *Lord Moyle*

Ballycastle Charters is one of the most established sea angling charter companies operating out of Ballycastle in Moyle, County Antrim, on the very north-eastern tip of Northern Ireland and runs a nine-metre Aqua-star sea fishing charter boat the *Lord Moyle*. Fishing trips take place along the Causeway Coast, Rathlin Island or over on the Scottish coast which is only 12 miles away. You can expect to catch coalfish, cod, conger, dab, flounder, gurnards, haddock, ling, pollack, pouting, scad, blue shark, ballan wrasse, cuckoo wrasse, turbot, brill and plaice here.

CONTACT: 00 44 28 20762074.

Bundoran Star

Bundoran Star is a state of the art Lochin 333, 385 HP and is owned and skippered by Patrick O'Doherty. The *Bundoran Star* operates in Donegal bay which has some of the best fishing in the country with a wide variety of species to be caught. Species caught during the 2006 season include shark, skate, tope, rays, turbot, conger, ling, cod, pollack, coley, gurnards, John Dory, plaice, flounder, dab, megrim, dog fish and wrasse – well over thirty species in all.

CONTACT: 00 353 74 9841017, 00 353 87 419 8323;
E-mail: info@bundoranstar.ie

The *Caitlín Marie*

The *Caitlín Marie* is a new 33-foot Vigilante sea angling vessel based in Kincasslagh harbour in Co. Donegal and is owned and skippered by Paul Mc Gonagle. Some of the best fishing grounds are only ten minutes away from Kincasslagh Pier and species include pollack, coalfish, ling, cod, turbot, brill, plaice, megrim, dab, mackerel, ballan and cuckoo wrasse, dogfish and conger. The Donegal coastline is littered with wrecks from the Spanish Armada and two world wars which can produce huge fish as do many of the reefs around the local islands of Owey and Arranmore. They also offer good shelter in poorer conditions allowing fishing to continue almost all year round.

CONTACT: 00 353 74 9543187; Mobile: 00 353 87 987 0266.

Carmel Olivia

The *Carmel Olivia* is a 38-foot Interceptor owned and skippered John & Michael O'Brien at is based at Magheroarty in Co. Donegal. This vessel fishes around Tory island, some of the best fishing grounds in Europe for the sea angler. Species caught regularly here include pollack, mackerel, cod, coalfish, haddock, whiting, ling, conger, blue shark, skates, rays, dogfish, bullhuss, pouting, wrasse, gurnard, turbot, brill and halibut.

CONTACT: 00 353 (0)74 9135635, 00 353 (0)87 6279789;
E-mail: carmelolivia@hotmail.com

Smoothhound

The *Smoothhound* is a 33-foot Vigilante and is owned and skippered by Richard Timoney and is based at Mullaghmore in Co. Sligo. Expect to catch a whole range of species in Donegal bay like coalfish, cod, conger, dab, flounder, gurnards, haddock, ling, pollack, pouting, scad, blue shark, ballan wrasse, cuckoo wrasse, turbot, brill and plaice here.

CONTACT: 00 353 (0)86 8380700; E-mail: oilwind@eircom.net

Caitlin Marie

Gemini II

The *Gemini II* is a 39-foot Cygnus Cyfish vessel owned by John McLaughlin and skippered by Des Mills. It's based at Culdaff in Co. Donegal. There are numerous wrecks which fish well as there has been minimal commercial fishing here due to the fast tides and deep water. Specimen size pollack, cod, coalfish, haddock, whiting, ling, conger, ray, dogfish, bull huss, pouting, wrasse, gurnard, megrim, turbot, brill, plaice and dab are all caught here.

CONTACT: 00 353 74 9379141, 00 353 87 6574551; E-mail:desmills@eircom.net.

Burtonport

I have fished all around the coast of this country and in some overseas venues but one venue that, for me, consistently out-fishes all others in terms of sheer numbers, quality and different species of fish is Burtonport in Co. Donegal. And judging by the growing number of anglers from all over Europe who come fishing here annually, I am not alone in my conclusion.

From the moment you drive through this small fishing village and down to the harbour you can almost imagine what this port would have looked like twenty years ago when it was one of the largest exporters of whitefish in the country. In the late 1980s large spurdog catches and salmon catches of several thousand fish were landed here every week, and whitefish were landed in boxes by the hundreds. But sadly those days are gone and only a skeleton fleet remains. Like many other ports around the country, Burtonport has gone from a whitefish to a shellfish port in a bid to stay alive in these un-certain times for the fishing industry. Under the direction of the Burtonport fishermen's co-op, most of the fishing fleet have diversified to catching edible crab, lobster, shrimp and velvet crab.

On a typical day at sea, drift fishing over reefs or rough ground is the method most commonly used here, but anchoring on the reefs or on the sand can also be very rewarding. In June and July the fishing is fantastic, pollack, coalies and wrasse being the most prolific. Ling, conger, dogfish, grey and red gurnards, thornback ray and most of the flatfish family are also abundant at this time of the year.

To go fishing out of Burtonport for a day during the summer months you will need a good selection of fresh and quality frozen baits to catch a variety of the fish mentioned. Fishing a long flowing trace with a fresh sand eel for pollack is the most popular choice among the local anglers. Sometimes changing the sand eel for a long thin strip of mackerel, a large ragworm, arti-ficial eel or a jelly worm can prove to be equally effective.

Alternatively, using a spinning rod with a leadhead and a jelly worm at-tached to it or spinning with a ball shot can also be a brilliant and very excit-ing way of enticing a pollack to strike. Small shore crab, mussels, ragworm or lugworm are needed for fishing ballan wrasse, grey and red gurnards and most of the flatfish family, and sometimes a cocktail of these baits tipped with

Aerial view of Burtonport harbour, Co. Donegal

fresh mackerel can take some beating. Mackerel caught on the morning of your trip is a must if you are targeting the powerful ling and conger on the reefs, with frozen mackerel coming in a poor second, although the dogfish and thornback ray seem to prefer it to the fresh mackerel.

Lugworms can be dug on most beaches at low water, with the occasional white ragworm making an appearance; mussels can also be collected at low water around the rocky coves. Razor fish is a bait that is commonly used by the local anglers at Burtonport and they have accounted for some good catches, including cod, ling, whiting and some large haddock. Unfortunately, ragworm is the only bait that is not available to dig locally, but is brought in from Dublin and Northern Ireland. The ragworms must be booked in advance to insure your supply for the day.

At present there are only two full time charter boats operating out of Burtonport, a 31-foot Mitchell called *Surose* and a 43-foot Aqua-Star called the *Loinnir*. In the past a party of anglers from the Larne and district club had an exceptional day's fishing out of Burtonport; they were using the trip as a league outing day for their club. The winner of the league outing had a staggering seventy-nine fish with second place taking seventy-five fish. Their catch was mostly pollack but some cod, and ling were also caught. During a species hunt Neil, the skipper of the *Loinnir* took a party of local anglers on a range of different fishing grounds around Arranmore island. An impressive twenty-two species were landed on board for the day; the list was as follows: mackerel, garfish, pollack, coalies, cod, ling, conger, lesser spotted dogfish, spurdog, grey gurnard, red gurnard, tub gurnard, cuckoo wrasse, ballan wrasse, whiting, pouting, thornback and blonde ray, dab, megrim, plaice and a bonus turbot.

Bluemouth rockfish have been caught several times on a reef offshore by a party of anglers. These fish are rare and are an unusual catch for the sea angler; they are normally associated with very deep water and usually only make an appearance in commercial fishermen's nets. Garfish, black bream, triggerfish, halibut, monkfish, torsk and sole are all regularly caught on trips out of this port. If you are coming to Burtonport with your family then why not take a trip aboard the super fast sightseeing vessel *Realt na Maidne*, where you can go whale, dolphin, seal or bird watching and see some stunning scenery around the islands.

CONTACT: Call Seamus on 00 353 87 317 1810
Web: www.arranmorecharters.com; E-mail: arranmorecharters@eircom.net

Finally, if you are staying in Burtonport village overnight or for several days, take time to sample the warmth and hospitality of the locals. I promise you, you will not regret it.

To get here / arranging a trip

Donegal airport (Aerfort Dhún na nGall) is situated in the top north-western corner of Ireland along the west coast of Donegal. Amidst breathtaking beauty etched with a multitude of beautiful bays and glorious sandy beaches, it is just forty minutes from Dublin. This is one of the most modern regional airports in Europe, with twice daily flights to Dublin and flights to Glasgow Prestwick with onward connections from there. Aerfort Dhún na nGall's staff will cater for your every need in a highly proficient and friendly manner that is unique to Donegal. Check out www.donegalairport.ie

Donegal airport (Aerfort Dhún na nGall)

You can create your own customised angling holiday on www.donegal-anglingholidays.com. This website contains maps and information on shore angling marks and locations for finding bait from Lough Foyle to Bundoran in Co. Donegal.

There are full listings and contact information for all the licensed charter vessels in the county, details of available offers and an interactive map showing the location of each charter vessel. You can book online directly with the provider or contact the vessel owner directly.

As well as information directed at the sea angler, the website also contains detailed information on game angling packages, accommodation and other activities in Donegal that might appeal to the angler and his or her family. It is well worth a visit.

For the travelling sea angler this region is noted for its unspoiled natural scenery, shaped over millennia by the relentless action of the mighty Atlantic ocean. Here you will find some of the highest cliffs in Europe, a dramatic rocky coastline leading into sheltered bays and numerous sandy beaches, many of which are protected by an array of accessible islands. Much of Donegal is still sparsely populated and remains one of the last true wildernesses in Europe.

It seems fitting that I conclude my writing about sea angling at my favourite location. Here I can go fishing on the reef just beside Mallagh rock in Arranmore bay almost anytime (weather permitting). Hopefully you have read this book and taken in some of what I have written, using it as a reference to improve your skills or as encouragement to take up sea angling. I guarantee that going sea angling for a day will give you a new perspective on life.

There's an old, and very true saying which goes: 'The worst day fishing is better than the best day working.'

John Rafferty

ANGLER FISH

Lophius piscatorius

SPECIMEN WEIGHT: 40 lbs

BEST LOCATION: Deep sandy gullies at the edge of sandbanks

BAIT: Whole sand eels or mackerel fillets

DESCRIPTION: The Anglerfish as its name suggests fishes for its prey by flicking a small white piece of skin on an antenna above its mouth. Smaller fish mistake the lure as food and once they are close enough the Angler fish attacks with its huge mouth at lightning speed.

BLACK SOLE

Solea solea

SPECIMEN WEIGHT: 2lbs

BEST LOCATION: Sandy areas of seabed

BAIT: Lugworms and ragworms

DESCRIPTION: As its name suggests it is the shape of a shoe sole. It is also known as black sole and the Dover sole. This is a nocturnal feeding flatfish that lives on a diet of molluscs, worms and crustaceans. Occasionally the sole is caught during very dull days when the water is heavily coloured.

BRILL

Scophthalmus rhombus

SPECIMEN WEIGHT: 5lbs

BEST LOCATION: Sandbanks

BAIT: Sandeels, lugworms and ragworms

DESCRIPTION: The body of a brill is less angular, thinner and more slender in shape, and its skin is smooth to the touch, compared to that of the turbot. Its upper dorsal fin extends right down over its eyes. The brill's coloration can vary greatly from one area to the next.

COALFISH

Pollachius virens

SPECIMEN WEIGHT: 15lbs

BEST LOCATION: Wrecks and reefs

BAIT: Sandeels and mackerel strips

DESCRIPTION: The coalfish is often mistaken for its close cousin the pollack. Although fairly similar in appearance, there is some distinct differences between both species. The lateral line on the coalfish is whitish in colour and fairly straight and its jaws are level.

COD

Gadus morhua

SPECIMEN WEIGHT: 20lbs

BEST LOCATION: Wrecks and reefs

BAIT: Squid, mackerel, lugworms, sand eels and peeler crabs

DESCRIPTION: Cod are often called the dustbins of the sea and have an enormous appetite, they will eat almost everything. Shellfish, sand eels and marine worms are the main baits used by anglers when trying to catch a cod. But cod that move offshore are more at home with a diet of fish.

CONGER EEL

Conger conger

SPECIMEN WEIGHT: 40lbs

BEST LOCATION: Wrecks and rocky out-crops

BAIT: Freshly caught mackerel

DESCRIPTION: The conger has one continuous dorsal fin, which runs the whole length of its body and is one of the largest fish that the sea angler is likely to encounter. These powerful fish can grow to over 250lbs and will fight all the way to the surface, swimming in a figure of eight before twisting up and down on the line.

DAB

Limanda limanda

SPECIMEN WEIGHT: 1.5lbs

BEST LOCATION: Sandy areas of seabed

BAIT: Lugworms and ragworms

DESCRIPTION: The dab is easily recognisable by rubbing its skin from tail to head; the skin which can be light brown to dark brown in colour feels very rough to the touch. Dabs are often caught two or three at a time.

DOGFISH, LESSER SPOTTED

Scyliorhinus caniculus

SPECIMEN WEIGHT: 3.25lbs

BEST LOCATION: Sandy areas of seabed

BAIT: Day-old mackerel pieces

DESCRIPTION: A member of the shark family the dogfish has an orange-brown back, a pale cream underside and has a vast array of small spots peppered over its back and sides. The dogfish's skin has a sand paper like texture to it.

SPURDOG

Squalus acanthias

SPECIMEN WEIGHT: 12lbs

BEST LOCATION: Reefs and wrecks

BAIT: Herring or mackerel steaks

DESCRIPTION: The spurdog has a typical shark outline and body shape and gets its name from the two extremely sharp spines of bone (spurs) present on its back at the front of each of its two dorsal fins. There is no anal fin present on this species.

RED GURNARD

Aspitrigla cuculus

SPECIMEN WEIGHT: 2lbs

BEST LOCATION: Sandy and stony seabed

BAIT: Sandeels, mackerel pieces and lugworms

DESCRIPTION: The red gurnards are almost tropical with their bright red colour. They are found all along the eastern Atlantic and throughout the Mediterranean at depths from 15 to 100 fathoms.

GREY GURNARD

Eutrigla gurnardus

SPECIMEN WEIGHT: 1.5lbs

BEST LOCATION: Areas of sandy seabed

BAIT: Lugworms and mackerel pieces

DESCRIPTION: The grey gurnard is the most common species of gurnard to be found around the Irish coast. Their odd triangular appearance is due to a large bony head, which is devoid of either skin or scales. Their body is short and thin and tapers quickly towards the forked tail.

TUB GURNARD

Trigla lucerna

SPECIMEN WEIGHT: 5lbs

BEST LOCATION: Sandy seabed

BAIT: Sandeels and mackerel pieces

DESCRIPTION: The tub gurnard is the biggest member of the gurnard family. There is some confusion at times between tub gurnard and large red gurnard, however the tub has a vivid bright blue border to the tip of the large pectoral fins, which is missing from that of the red gurnard.

HADDOCK

Melanogrammus aeglifinus

SPECIMEN WEIGHT: 7lbs

BEST LOCATION: Sand and muddy bottoms

BAIT: Mussels, razorfish and lugworms

DESCRIPTION: The haddock can be identified by its slightly forked tail, black lateral line and a dark spot on either side of its body, just below the lateral line and above the pectoral fin. This spot, as the tale goes, was caused by St. Peter's thumb when he lifted the fish out of the sea.

LING

Molva molva

SPECIMEN WEIGHT: 25lbs

BEST LOCATION: Reefs and wrecks

BAIT: Mackerel fillets

DESCRIPTION: The ling is a member of the cod family. Although slightly similar in size and shape the ling is easily distinguishable from the conger; they are brighter in colour and have two dorsal fins. The first one is short and the second dorsal fin runs down the rest of the back and stops at the wrist of the tail.

MACKEREL

Scomber scombrus

SPECIMEN WEIGHT: 2.5lbs

BEST LOCATION: Wrecks and reefs

BAIT: Feathers or pieces of sandeel

DESCRIPTION: The mackerel has magnificent markings all along its back and is covered by dark stripes intermingled with iridescent blue and green stripes. The coloured flanks are also iridescent and the belly is a silvery white. Mackerel is streamlined and hydro-dynamically shaped for lightning bursts of speed.

MEGRIM

Lepidorhombus whiffiagonis

SPECIMEN WEIGHT: 1.75lbs

BEST LOCATION: Muddy and mixed sand bottom

BAIT: Lugworm, razorfish and mackerel pieces

DESCRIPTION: An oval left-sided flatfish, which has large eyes and mouth. It is pale yellow and almost translucent in colour on its upper surface. Scales on its blind side are smooth.

PLAICE

Pleuronectes platessa

SPECIMEN WEIGHT: 4lbs

BEST LOCATION: Sandy bottom close to mussel beds

BAIT: Mussels, razorfish and lugworms

DESCRIPTION: The plaice has a powerful oval body with bright orange to light red spots. Its eyes and coloured half are on the right side of the body and like most fish the colours vary slightly from one area to the next. The scales on the plaice are so small and so well embedded in the skin, that the skin feels very smooth to the touch.

POLLACK

Pollachius pollachius

SPECIMEN WEIGHT: 12lbs

BEST LOCATION: Wreck and reefs

BAIT: Sandeels and ragworms

DESCRIPTION: The pollack is a powerful predatory fish that has large eyes, golden-green, bronze flanks, tiny scales and a big mouth with small sharp teeth and a protruding bottom jaw. Bigger fish are found around wrecks and reefs in deeper water.

BLONDE RAY

Raja brachyura

SPECIMEN WEIGHT: 25lbs

BEST LOCATION: Sandy seabeds

BAIT: Sandeels and mackerel pieces

DESCRIPTION: The blonde ray is light brown in colour has a few lighter blotches with a heavy scattering of dark spots all the way to the tail and to the tips of each wing. The underside is creamy white. The body is slightly less angular and does not possess the razor sharp thorns that the thornback ray has.

THORNBACK RAY

Raja clavata

SPECIMEN WEIGHT: 20lbs

BEST LOCATION: Sandy seabeds

BAIT: Sandeels and mackerel pieces

DESCRIPTION: The thornback ray has a diamond-shaped body with two dorsal fins almost at the tip of the tail, the tail itself is ringed with a distinctive black banding and the underside of the body is a creamy white colour. As its name implies it has a number of thorny spines on the back and tail.

BLUE SHARK

Prionace glauca

SPECIMEN WEIGHT: 100lbs

BEST LOCATION: Off rocky headlands during September

BAIT: Freshly caught mackerel

DESCRIPTION: The blue shark is a powerful but slender fish with large wing-like pectoral fins. Its colour is a dark blue dorsally and a vivid blue on both sides, which soon fades if the fish is out of the water for any period of time.

PORBEAGLE

Lamna nasus

SPECIMEN WEIGHT: 150lbs

BEST LOCATION: Off rocky headlands and over deep water wrecks

BAIT: Freshly caught mackerel

DESCRIPTION: The porbeagle is a cold water shark and spends most of the year around our coast. This is a heavy bodied shark with most of its bulk above its pectoral fins making this a true big game species.

TOPE

Galeorhinus galeus

SPECIMEN WEIGHT: 40lbs

BEST LOCATION: Rathmullan and Carlingford lough

BAIT: Freshly caught mackerel

DESCRIPTION: The tope has a slender shark-like appearance with a long pointed snout, large pectoral fins and a large mouth with sharp triangular teeth. It has two dorsal fins, one large and one small, and five prominent gill slits on each side. The large tail has a deeply notched upper lobe and the fish has a greyish, bronze to taupe coloured upper body and paler undersides.

TORSK

Brosme brosme

SPECIMEN WEIGHT: 6lbs

BEST LOCATION: Wrecks and deepwater reefs

BAIT: Musels, crab and mackerel pieces

DESCRIPTION: Found in small shoals on rough, rock, gravel, or pebble bottoms. Generally found far from the shore and around deep water shipwrecks. The torsk has a barbel on its chin. Its colour is variable; dorsally dark red-brown or green brown to yellow shading into a paler colour on its belly.

TURBOT

Scophthalmus maximus

SPECIMEN WEIGHT: 18lbs

BEST LOCATION: Sandbanks

BAIT: Live or fresh whole sand eels

DESCRIPTION: The turbot is oval in shape and the surface of its back is covered with hard bony tubercles, which makes it feel very rough to the touch. The coloration on its back is normally a greyish-brown with a thick freckling of darker spots and blotches.

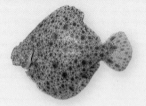

WHITING

Merlangius merlangus

SPECIMEN WEIGHT: 3lbs

BEST LOCATION: mud, gravel, sand and stony bottoms

BAIT: Small sprat, sand eels, lugworms, squid and mackerel pieces

DESCRIPTION: The coloration of the whiting is quite variable in certain areas from a yellowish – brown to a dark blue or green and often with a small dark blotch at the upper base of the pectoral fin. The whiting also has a tooth filled mouth.

BALLAN WRASSE

Labrus bergylta

SPECIMEN WEIGHT: 4.75lbs

BEST LOCATION: Rocky outcrops and shallow reefs

BAIT: Ragworms, lugworms and small hardback crabs

DESCRIPTION: The ballan wrasse has a large scaled body, a mouthful of extremely sharp teeth and a long spiny dorsal fin. The coloration of the ballan wrasse is extremely variable, from a deep brown to green to a freckled red.

CUCKOO WRASSE

Labrus mixtus

SPECIMEN WEIGHT: 1.25lbs

BEST LOCATION: Shallow reefs and rocky seabeds

BAIT: Small sandeels, mackerel pieces and crustaceans

DESCRIPTION: The cuckoo wrasse is without a doubt our most colourful fish. Females and immature males, tend to be a yellowish brown to red colour. But mature males have vivid bright blue heads and sides with a bright orange/yellow underbelly.

FISH NAMES IN ENGLISH

FISH NAMES IN IRISH

English	Irish
Angler fish	Láimhíneach
Bass	Bas
Black sole	Sól Dubh
Bluemouth rockfish	Iasc carraige an bhéil ghoirm
Brill	Broit
Coalfish	Glasán
Cod	Trosc
Conger eel	Eascann choncair
Dab	Scarbhóg (U) leith gharbh
Spurdog	Gobóg (U) Fíogach gobach
Greater spotted dogfish (Bull huss)	Madadh scadán (U) Fíogach mór
Lesser spotted dogfish	Dallóg (U) Fíogach beag
Flounder	Leith
Garfish	Corr uaine
Tub gurnard	Cnúdán gorm
Grey gurnard	Cnúdán glas
Red gurnard	Cnúdán dearg
Haddock	Cadóg
Hake	Colmoir
Halibut	Haileabó
Herring	Scadán
John Dory	Deóraí
Ling	Beithíoch an éisc mhóir (U), Langa
Mackerel	Marlas (U), Ronnach, Maicréal
Megrim	Méagram
Monkfish	Iasc manaigh (U), Iasc na n-eiteog (U), láimhíneach

Grey mullet	Lannach
Golden grey mullet	Lannach glas
Red mullet	Lannach dearg
Plaice	Leith bhallánach (U), leathóg bhallach
Pollack	Deargóg (U), Súilín (U), mangach.
Pouting	Cáitín
Thornback ray	Sciata garbh (U), roc garbh
Blonde ray	Sciata fionn
Sting ray	Sciata an gha nimhe
Cuckoo ray	Sciata na súl dubh, roc na súl dubh
Undulate ray	Sciata dústríoctha
Homelyn ray	Sciata bhallánach (U), roc mín, rotha Mhín
Painted ray	Sciata daite
Electric ray	Craimpiasc
Ray's bream	Sáimhín
Red sea bream	Garbhánach (U), deargán, sléibhín
Twaite shad	Sead fhallacsach
Porbeagle shark	Craosaire
Blue shark	Beáthach gorm (U), siorc gorm
Six gilled shark	Siorc liath
Common skate	Sciata, scolabard
White skate	Sciata bán
Sand eel	Corr (U), scadán gainimh, spéirlint
Scad	Bolmán, scadán carraige, gabhar
Smooth hound	Madadh glas (U), sciorneach
Stone basse	Breac raice
Three bearded rockling	Donnán trí ribe
Tope	Madadh gorm (U), gearrthóir, gobóg

Torsk	Torsca, tusc
Trigger fish	Iasc truicir
Turbot	Turbard, scolabard
Albacore tuna	Tuinnín
Bluefin tuna	Tuinnín gorm
Whiting	Feannóg (U), Foitín
Ballan wrasse	Ballán (U), Ballach
Cuckoo wrasse	An Dochtúir (U), Ballach Muire, Splanc, Deargadh bear
Mussel	Sliogán dhubh, diúilicín, iascán
Green crab	Glasphortán
Peeler crab	Snámhaí
Clam	Breallach
Razor fish	Scian mhara
Cockle	Ruacan
Winkle	Fuitheog (U), Faocha
Limpet	Bairneach
Barnacle	Giúrann
Squid	Máthair shúigh
Sprat	Maghar, salán
Lugworm	Slugach (U), lugach
Ragworm	Raga, Ruarámhach

* (U) = Ulster Irish version of the fish names where it is different to the other dialects.

Glossary

2/0, 3/0, 4/0, 6/0 ETC: different hook sizes.

ANAL FIN: located on the ventral surface behind the anus.

BAIT ELASTIC: a very thin thread like elastic that is used for securing soft baits onto hooks.

BAIT FISH: small fish that are hunted by bigger fish.

BEADS: small plastic balsl with a hole in the middle which line is passed through.

BLANK: a rod without its fittings, i.e. rings.

BLOODY BUTCHER: an artificial fly used in freshwater fishing.

BOOM / WIRE BOOM: used for keeping your trace from tangling on your mainline and for attaching the weight.

BOTTOM FEEDING FISH: fish that search for their food on the seabed.

BRAID: a type of fishing line that is far stronger and much thinner than conventional line. It offers less resistance in the water therefore lighter weights can be used.

COCKTAIL: a mix of several baits used at the same time.

CONGER TRACE: a wire trace with at least a 10/0 hook attached to it.

CREELS: also known as pots and traps and are used by commercial fishermen for catching crabs and lobsters.

CRIMPS: small metal sleeves that are slid onto the line and are then squeezed to hold them in place.

DACRON: a woven thread line which is now being surpassed by the newer braids.

DOUBLE SPREADER: a boom that has two snoods attached at both ends and a swivel and weight link in the centre, this type of boom is generally used for flat fishing.

DRAG: the braking system on your reel which can be use for applying tension to a fighting fish.

DROPPERS: also called snoods, these are the short pieces of line that hang out from the main body of your trace that hooks are attached to.

FATHOM: equal to six feet.

FIXED SPOOL REEL: where the spool does not move and a bail arm lays the line on the spool. This type of reel is generally used for spinning.

FLOWING TRACE: a trace which can be anywhere form a few inches in length up to 18 feet or so. This trace is attached to the boom and runs horizontally to your mainline.

FOUL HOOKED: when the fish is hooked outside the mouth or on the body.

FREE SPOOL: when the spool can run freely going forward or in reverse.

FREE-LINING: where your trace is released into the water without any weight and the bait or lure is allowed to sink naturally.

HIGH AND LOW WATER: when the tide has come in or gone out and reached its highest or lowest mark.

HOKKAIS: a type of feathered trace.

HOLLOW PLASTIC BOOM: lets you run your line through the boom.

HOOK-UPS: when you strike with your rod by lifting it and firmly set the hook in the fish's mouth.

JELLY WORMS: artificial plastic worm-shaped lures that move like fish when pulled through the water.

JIGGING: when a jig type lure is fished by lifting the rod then lowering it to give the lure movement.

JOEY MACKEREL: juvenile mackerel.

LEAD BALL SHOT: a ball of lead with a hole through its centre.

LEAD HEAD: a hook with moulded lead on its eye and is used in conjunction with a jelly worm for spinning.

LEVER DRAG: a superior braking system on your fishing reel compared to the older star drag system.

LING TRACE: either a heavy mono or a wire trace with a 6/0 or bigger hook attached

MACKEREL FLAPPERS: where the backbone is removed from the mackerel but the fillets are still attached to the head of the fish.

MACKEREL STRIPS: cutlets of flesh from the Mackerel's body.

MID-WATER: halfway between the seabed and the surface.

MONO: monofilament is the fishing line you put on your reel or what your traces are tied with.

MULTIPLIER REEL: a type of reel where the line drum rotates faster that the handle.

MUPPET: an artificial lure shaped like a squid

ONE UP AND TWO DOWN: a description of a type of trace. The one up two down trace consists of one snood above a weight and a boom and two snoods off the boom.

PECTORAL FINS: placed behind the gill slits.

PEELER CRABS: crabs that are moulting their shells.

PIRK: a chrome finished lure that has a hook/hooks on one end and a swivel on the other. The pirk also acts as a weight. The first pirk type lures were invented by Scandinavian fishermen for catching cod, ling and pollack and were made with shiny lead covered with hooks – this was known as a ripper.

POOR COD: a fish much like a pouting.

RATCHET: the ratchet on a reel stops the spool from over running, the ratchet can be selected by a small knob which is located on the side of the spool.

ROD RINGS: the rings that the fishing line runs through on a rod.

RUBBY DUBBY BAG: an onion sack or similar type bag that is filled with chopped up mackerel and fish oil, hung over the side of the boat and is used to attract sharks.

RUNNING BOOM: slides up and down on the mainline.

RUNNING LEGER RIG: allows the fish to take the baited hook and move away freely, as the line will slide away from the weight. The bite is easily felt and the fish should feel little resistance.

SHOCK LEADER: a length of heavier mono that acts as a shock absorber when casting your trace out.

SLACK WATER: when the tide has gone out to it fullest and will soon begin to come back in again.

SLIDING FLOAT RIG: The sliding float is attached to the mainline and can slide up and down the line to any depth. The depth is set by applying a stop knot to the mainline.

SNAP SWIVEL: a quicker system of attaching the swivel to your line.

SNOOD: a piece of line that hangs clear of the trace.

SPECIMEN WEIGHT: a designated weight given to each fish by the Irish Specimen Fish Committee. Any fish over that weight is deemed an exception catch and is merited with a certificate by the ISFC.

SPINNING WITH PLUGS: an artificial but realistic looking lure that is cast out and reeled in at speed.

SPOON / SONAR TYPE SPOON: chrome plated disks that are used as fish attractors on your traces.

STAR DRAG SYSTEM: the reel's braking system that is set by a star shaped wheel located under the handle.

STOP KNOT: used to stop the sliding float at a pre-determined depth. The knot is usually a separate piece of line or power gum that is tied on the mainline.

STRIKE: when you feel a fish and you lift your rod to set the hook in the fish's mouth.

SWIM BLADDER an internal organ that contributes to the ability of a fish to control its buoyancy.

SWIVEL: keeps take the twists out of your line while you are fishing.

THREE-UP METHOD: this is your standard trace, a three-up rig is a trace with three snoods and hooks/lures and the weight hangs at the bottom of the trace.

TIDAL RACE: where the incoming or outgoing tide is forced between two islands or a narrow gap. Because of the volume of water trying to get through, the speed of the tide increases.

TRACES: Traces are the end rigs for catching fish, they normally consist of three snoods on which the hooks are tied. Sometimes beads, feathers and/or spoons are attached to traces as attractors.

TROLLING A LURE: where a lure is towed behind a boat at a pre-determined speed.

TUBI-BOOM: a hollow boom that the mainline runs through.

TWO UP AND ONE DOWN: a trace where the two up are two snoods and hooks above the weight and boom and the one down is another snood that runs off behind the boom.

UPTIDING ROD: when the boat is anchored and your bait is cast up-tide from the boat.

VHF: stands for very high frequency. It is the radio frequency range from 30 MHz to 300 MHz and is used for marine communications.

MERCIER PRESS

Douglas Village, Cork

www.mercierpress.ie

Trade enquiries to Columba Mercier Distribution,
55a Spruce Avenue, Stillorgan Industrial Park, Blackrock, Dublin

978 1 85635 553 7

10 9 8 7 6 5 4 3 2 1

 Mercier Press receives financial assistance from
the Arts Council/An Chomhairle Ealaíon

Printed & bound in Spain by GraphyCems, Villatuerta, Navarra